THE
GOOD DEED

GUIDE

Library of Congress Cataloging in Publication
Number: 2002094027

ISBN: 1-931686-33-5

Printed in Singapore

Typeset in Engravers and Officina Sans

Designed by Bryn Ashburn

Distributed in North America by Chronicle Books
85 Second Street
San Francisco, CA 94105

10 9 8 7 6 5 4 3 2 1

Quirk Books
215 Church Street
Philadelphia, PA 19106
www.quirkbooks.com

THE
GOOD DEED
GUIDE

SIMPLE WAYS TO MAKE THE WORLD A BETTER PLACE

BY JAMES & LISA GRACE

ILLUSTRATIONS BY ALEXANDER STADLER

QUIRK BOOKS

PHILADELPHIA

CONTENTS

INTRODUCTION

> *"The greatest mistake of all is to do nothing*
> *if you can only do a little."*
>
> —Sir John Golding

More and more these days, you can't pick up a newspaper without being struck by the problems of the world. There is war, hunger, and greed. You may read all this and wring your hands. It *is* overwhelming.

But if you don't become too discouraged and you read beyond the front page, you will also find something more: tales of courage, compassion, generosity, humor, and love. For every bit of sadness, you will find an equal amount of hope, and it all emanates from the simple acts of kindness performed by people the world over.

You too can be a force of good in the world, if you choose to. You can brighten the day of those around you through simple good deeds. You can decide to send goodness out into the world—not just by what you think or what you say, but by what you do. You don't need to wear a cape and tights to be a hero. You simply need to decide not to sit on the sidelines.

The Good Deed Guide is your road map to taking an active part in changing the world for the better. The chapters that follow provide the first steps for reaching out to friends and neighbors, caring for strangers, administering first aid to people—and animals—in need, and doing good works in your community.

The choice is yours. Make a difference. Do good.

DOING GOOD WITH
FIRST AID

HOW TO HELP AN INJURED BIRD

Birds play an important role in the delicate balance between man and nature, but a sad fact of life is: Birds get hurt. They fly into windows, they fly in front of cars, they get caught by cats. One day, you may come upon a bird in need. It is important to know what to do.

1 **CAREFULLY EXAMINE THE INJURED BIRD.** Try to determine whether the bird is alive. Can you see its breast rising and falling? If it is alive, look for any obvious injuries and proceed to step 2. If the bird has died, bury it in a shady, well-protected spot.

2 **LINE AN UNWAXED PAPER BAG OR CARDBOARD BOX WITH TISSUES OR PAPER TOWELS.** Bring the bag or box outside next to the bird. If you are using a paper bag, poke some holes near the opening. Fold over the opening to secure the bird, making sure it has enough air. If you're using a cardboard box, poke a few holes in its sides. (Fig. A)

> *Some people believe that a bird handled by a human will be rejected by its parents. Not so. Birds don't have a highly developed sense of smell and therefore do not recognize the sensory cues that humans leave behind.*

3 PUT ON GLOVES. This will protect your fingers in case the bird pecks at you.

4 CAREFULLY PICK UP THE BIRD. Scoop the bird gently into your hands. Keep its head well-supported.

5 GENTLY PLACE THE BIRD IN THE PREPARED BAG OR BOX. (Fig. B)

6 KEEP THE BIRD UPRIGHT. If it cannot sit up on its own, create a "donut cushion" out of a piece of tissue and position the bird on top of it.

fig. A | pokes holes in the sides of a box

fig. B | gently place the bird in the box

As much as you may want to, don't give the injured bird anything to eat or drink. Many well-intentioned people mistakenly give birds things that they shouldn't eat. Sometimes the bird doesn't even recognize the offering as food (e.g., bird seed for an owl); other times the food offered is toxic to the bird (e.g., avocados and many fruits with pits). Even water can be harmful to a bird in large quantities—the bird may drown in it.

Don't offer the bird anything to eat or drink unless specifically instructed to do so by a wildlife rehabilitator.

7 **FOLD CLOSED THE PAPER BAG, OR FOLD DOWN THE FLAPS OF THE BOX.** Place a book over the flaps of the box to keep them down. If left uncovered, the stunned bird may recover and fly around inside your home.

8 **IF THE BIRD'S INJURIES ARE SERIOUS, CALL A WILDLIFE REHABILITATOR.** If the bird is bleeding or if its wing is broken, the rehabilitator will instruct you on how to treat the bird.

9 **PLACE THE BOX IN A QUIET, DARK PLACE.** Leave the bird undisturbed for an hour or two.

10 **CHECK ON THE BIRD.** If the bird is alert and trying to get out of the bag or box, it is ready to be let go.

11 **RETURN THE BIRD TO THE WORLD.** Carry the box or bag outside and carefully open it. If the bird flies out on its own, great! If not, gently pick it up and set it down on the ground. Touch the bird as little as possible. Don't throw the bird into the air. This "launching" will disorient it.

HOW TO PREVENT BIRD INJURIES

1 *CATS EAT BIRDS—IT'S AS SIMPLE AS THAT.* Keep your cat indoors or in a screened enclosure so that it can't reach any birds.

2 *KEEP PESTICIDE USE TO A MINIMUM.* Birds that feed on grasses and seeds coated in pesticides can get very sick, or even die.

3 *BE MINDFUL OF WHERE YOU PLACE BIRD FEEDERS.* Place bird feeders either on the house itself or at least ten feet away from the house. Birds can easily judge the distance to a house itself, but if the feeder is within that ten-foot margin, they may have trouble distinguishing between it and the house and end up hitting the house or the feeder.

WHAT TO DO IF YOU FIND A LOST BABY BIRD

If you stumble upon a baby bird, your instinct may be to take it in and care for it on your own. Your heart is in the right place, but don't do it! Baby birds cared for by humans often die of malnutrition or from improper care. Even though a fledgling looks unkempt or as if it can't make it on its own, its parents most likely know exactly where their little one is and will return for it. However, there are times a baby may need help to return to its family:

★ **IF THE BABY BIRD DOES NOT HAVE ALL ITS FEATHERS BUT APPEARS HEALTHY, IT HAS PROBABLY FALLEN FROM THE NEST.** *Gently place the bird back in the nest, if you can find it.*

★ **IF YOU SEE THE NEST ON THE GROUND, IT MAY HAVE FALLEN WITH THE BABY IN IT.** *Try to place the nest back where it came from. Check nearby bushes, trees, and gutters for signs of remaining twigs, straw, or other clues to the nest's original location. Stabilize the nest, then place the baby back in it.*

★ **IF YOU CAN'T FIND THE NEST BUT HAVE AN IDEA WHERE IT WAS LOCATED, MAKE A SURROGATE NEST.** *Find an empty margarine tub or a similar container, fill it with grass or leaves from the area, nail it to a nearby tree, and place the baby bird in it. The parents will find it.*

★ **ONCE YOU'VE PLACED THE BIRD IN ITS NEST, CHECK ON IT FROM AFAR.** *Don't keep approaching the nest, or the parents may become too nervous to return. If the parents have not come back after several hours, call the humane society for help.*

HOW TO TREAT A CHILD'S SKINNED KNEE

Though it may rank low on the list of major injuries, a child's skinned knee can really hurt.

1 DRY THE CHILD'S TEARS AND OFFER A HUG.

2 TAKE A LOOK TO SEE HOW BAD IT IS. If the wound is bleeding a lot and there seems to be a deep cut, seek medical attention. If the wound has only a little bit of bleeding from a small cut or abrasion, treat it yourself.

3 RINSE THE WOUND THOROUGHLY WITH WATER TO CLEAN OUT THE DIRT.

4 WASH THE WOUND WITH A MILD SOAP AND RINSE THOROUGHLY. Avoid antiseptic solutions, which don't provide any additional protection. (Fig. A)

5 COVER THE WOUND WITH ANTIBACTERIAL OINTMENT AND A STERILE ADHESIVE BANDAGE OR STERILE GAUZE AND ADHESIVE TAPE. A big Band-Aid will do. (Figs. B, C)

6 KISS THE BOO-BOO. (Fig. D)

Fig. A | wash the wound gently

Fig. B | coat the wound with anti-bacterial ointment

Fig. C | cover the wound with an adhesive bandage

Fig. D | kiss the boo-boo

7 **LOOK AT THE KNEE EVERY DAY.** If the bandage gets wet, remove it and apply a new one. After the scrape or cut forms a scab, a bandage is no longer necessary.

8 **CALL YOUR CHILD'S DOCTOR IF THE WOUND IS RED, SWOLLEN, TENDER, WARM, OR BEGINNING TO DRAIN.**

HOW TO REMOVE A
SPLINTER

Splinters can happen just about anywhere—and when they do, it's best to be prepared with a pair of tweezers and/or a needle, depending on the severity. There's an art to removing splinters, but once you've mastered it you'll have the power to save countless others from suffering needless pain.

1 LOOK AT THE SKIN CAREFULLY. Determine whether the splinter is sticking out of the skin.

2 IF THE SPLINTER IS STICKING OUT OF THE SKIN, GRAB IT AT THE BASE WITH A PAIR OF TWEEZERS. Pull the splinter straight out. Be careful not to break a piece off, leaving the rest of it embedded in the skin.

Note: If you don't have tweezers or a needle handy, reach for tape of any kind. Simply put the tape over the splinter, then pull it off. Tape removes most splinters painlessly and easily.

3 IF THE SPLINTER IS ALREADY DEEP WITHIN THE SKIN, PREPARE TO REMOVE IT WITH A NEEDLE. This is the part that hurts. If the splinter victim is a child, you may need another person to provide comfort and hold the child while you remove the splinter.

4 SOAK THE AFFECTED AREA IN WARM WATER FOR A FEW MINUTES TO SOFTEN THE SKIN. (Fig. A)

5 WIPE A NEEDLE AND TWEEZERS WITH RUBBING ALCOHOL TO STERILIZE THEM. (Fig. B)

6 USE THE NEEDLE TO GENTLY SLIT THE SURFACE OF THE SKIN RIGHT OVER THE SPLINTER. (Fig. C)

7 CAREFULLY USE THE TWEEZERS TO REMOVE THE SPLINTER. (Fig. D)

Don't worry if you can't get the splinter out. Over a few days the splinter should work itself out. In the meantime, watch for signs of infection, including pus, redness, and swelling. If the area gets infected, call a health care provider. (Infections from splinters are quite rare, however.)

8 WASH THE WHOLE AREA THOROUGHLY WITH SOAP AND WARM WATER.

9 COVER THE SPOT WITH A THIN FILM OF ANTIBIOTIC OINTMENT AND A BANDAGE.

10 KISS THE BOO BOO. . . . And make time for a big hug.

Fig. A | soak the affected area in warm water

Fig. B | sterilize the tweezers and needle

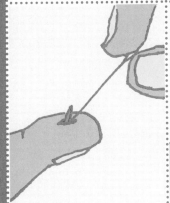

Fig. C | gently slit the skin with the needle

Fig. D | remove the splinter using the tweezers

HOW TO CURE HICCUPS

The end of the world? No. Annoying? Yes. Curing another person's hiccups will gain you much respect, and a lot of thanks.

1 ASSESS THE SITUATION. In some cases, hiccups indicate the need for medical attention. If the hiccups occur in association with another illness, such as a prolonged cough, muscle weakness on one side of the body, severe vomiting, or very bad stomach pain, medical attention is warranted. If the hiccups last for days or if the hiccups started after taking prescription medication, get medical attention.

THE HICCUP IN HISTORY

Plato quotes an exchange between the playwright Aristophanes and the physician Eryximachus that took place sometime around 400 B.C. The playwright asked the physician to heal his hiccups. "Let me recommend that you hold your breath," responded Eryximachus, "and if this fails, gargle with a little water; and if the hiccup still continues, tickle your nose with something and sneeze, and if you sneeze once or twice, even the most violent hiccup is sure to go."

2 IF IT IS MERELY A RUN-OF-THE-MILL CASE OF THE HICCUPS, TRY EACH OF THESE TRIED AND TRUE METHODS UNTIL YOU FIND ONE THAT WORKS. (Don't try to scare the person. It doesn't work and you end up looking silly.)

* Have the hiccuper drink from the far side of a glass of water while bent over. (Fig. A)
* Have the hiccuper hold his or her breath for as long as possible. (Fig. B)
* Have the hiccuper take ten sips of water all in one breath.

3 IF NONE OF THESE WORKS, OR IF THEY'RE TOO DIFFICULT TO ATTEMPT, TRY SOME SWEETNESS. This is especially helpful with children. Mary Poppins sang, "Just a spoonful of sugar helps the medicine go down." Following her advice, administer one teaspoon of sugar or peanut butter. (Fig. C) Have the hiccuper swallow it fast. If the hiccups don't stop right away, do it three or more times, once every two minutes. (Note: For younger children, use one teaspoon of corn syrup. After each dose of sugar, lay the child down for a few minutes.)

4 LET HICCUPPING BABIES BE. For the most part, leave a hiccupping baby alone. Give the baby a bottle of water if it makes you feel better. Some doctors think that hiccups may be brought on by overstimulation. If you notice the baby hiccupping during a particularly stimulating activity, you may want to decrease or eliminate that activity.

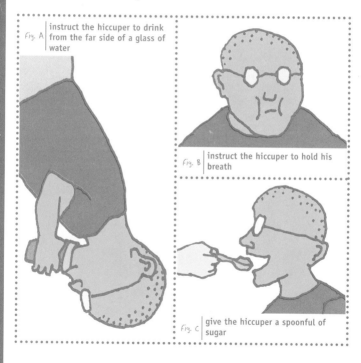

fig. A | instruct the hiccuper to drink from the far side of a glass of water

fig. B | instruct the hiccuper to hold his breath

fig. C | give the hiccuper a spoonful of sugar

HOW TO SAVE SOMEONE
WHO IS CHOKING

What would you do if the person next to you were choking? She can't speak, she can barely breathe. She is looking to you for help. The situation is even more desperate when the victim is a very young child, who will not be able to communicate her distress.

Knowing how to save a person who is choking is an important lifesaving skill. If you've already learned this skill, it couldn't hurt to remind yourself of the steps; if you've never learned this skill, read the following steps very carefully. Then read them again.

If the victim is coughing, speaking, or breathing, this indicates that the person is in the process of fixing the problem already. You may want to bring her a glass of water to soothe her irritated throat after all the coughing. If the person cannot cough, speak, or breathe, proceed with the Heimlich Maneuver.

PERFORMING THE HEIMLICH MANEUVER ON OTHERS

1 STAND BEHIND THE VICTIM AND WRAP YOUR ARMS AROUND HER WAIST. Bend the victim slightly forward.

2 **MAKE A FIST WITH ONE HAND AND PLACE IT BELOW THE RIBCAGE AND SLIGHTLY ABOVE THE VICTIM'S BELLY BUTTON.** Turn your fist so that the knuckle of your thumb is against the choking victim's body.

3 **GRASP YOUR FIST WITH THE OTHER HAND.** Press against the choking victim hard with a quick, upward thrust. Repeat this until the object

perform the Heimlich Manuever until the object is expelled

is expelled from the airway. If done correctly, the object should be expelled with the first thrust. If after three attempts the object is still in the person's throat, seek professional medical attention.

4 **ENCOURAGE THE VICTIM TO GET TO A HOSPITAL AS SOON AS POSSIBLE TO MAKE SURE NO DAMAGE WAS DONE.**

PERFORMING THE MANEUVER ON AN INFANT OR TODDLER
If the person who is choking is an infant or a toddler up

to one year of age, the child may not be able to indicate what is wrong with him. If the child has stopped breathing, is turning blue, or appears to be experiencing extreme discomfort, modify the Heimlich in the following way. Be very gentle.

1 SIT DOWN.

2 SIT THE CHILD ON YOUR LAP, FACING AWAY FROM YOU AND LEANING OVER YOUR FOREARM.

3 USE THE HEEL OF YOUR OTHER HAND TO GIVE FOUR LIGHT AND RAPID BLOWS BETWEEN THE SHOULDER BLADES. Repeat two or three times. The object should be expelled.

4 IF THIS DOESN'T WORK, TURN THE CHILD ON HIS OR HER BACK ACROSS YOUR LAP.

5 PUT YOUR FINGERS ON THE CHILD'S BREAST-BONE JUST BELOW THE NIPPLES.

lay the child down and perform a modified Heimlich Maneuver

WHAT DO I DO IF THE CHOKING VICTIM PASSES OUT?

The following technique is also useful when the choking person is substantially bigger than you and you can't position your arms around him or her.

1 *PLACE THE VICTIM ON HIS OR HER BACK.*

2 *STRADDLE THE VICTIM'S HIPS SO YOU ARE FACING HIS OR HER HEAD.*

3 *WITH ONE HAND ON TOP OF THE OTHER, PLACE THE HEEL OF YOUR BOTTOM HAND ON THE UPPER ABDOMEN, BELOW THE RIB CAGE AND ABOVE THE BELLY BUTTON.*

4 *USE YOUR BODY WEIGHT TO PRESS INTO THE VICTIM'S UPPER ABDOMEN WITH A QUICK UPWARD THRUST.*

5 *REPEAT UNTIL THE OBJECT IS EXPELLED.*

6 *IF THE PERSON DOES NOT RECOVER, PROCEED WITH CPR. Do this only if you've been properly trained. You can get training in any number of places; simply call your local hospital for information. Don't delay!*

6 DEPRESS THE CHILD'S CHEST ONE AND ONE-HALF INCHES. Do this quickly four times.

7 IF THIS DOES NOT EXPEL THE OBJECT, REPEAT STEP 3.

8 TAKE THE CHILD TO A HOSPITAL AS SOON AS POSSI-
BLE. Even if you expel the object, take the child to
the hospital to make sure no damage has been done.
When the child is older, teach him or her the universal
gesture for choking (both hands lightly grasping one's
throat) so that the child can quickly communicate a
problem.

HOW TO MAKE CHICKEN SOUP FOR A SICK FRIEND

Your friend has a cold and feels miserable. His nose hurts, his head hurts, and all he wants to do is curl up in bed and be pampered a little. What can comfort your sick friend better than a batch of homemade chicken soup?

Although there are millions of chicken soup recipes, here is a simple, traditional soup sure to warm anyone's heart. This recipe serves four to six people, and it takes about two hours to prepare.

1 ASSEMBLE YOUR INGREDIENTS.
You will need:
2 quarts of water
1 whole 3-pound chicken, washed and quartered
1 large white onion, peeled and cut into wedges
4 peeled carrots, cut into 1-inch pieces
4 stalks celery, cut into 1-inch pieces

2 COMBINE THE WATER AND CHICKEN PARTS IN A LARGE SOUP POT. (Fig. A)

3 BRING TO JUST UNDER A BOIL, THEN LOWER HEAT.

Simmer slowly for approximately 30 to 40 minutes, skimming as needed. (Fig. B)

4 **WHEN THE CHICKEN IS COOKED THOROUGHLY, REMOVE IT FROM THE POT.** Set the pieces aside to cool. You'll know it is cooked thoroughly when the meat has no traces of pink. (Fig. C)

5 **ADD THE VEGETABLES TO THE BROTH.**

TRUE "COMFORT FOOD"

Scientists have confirmed what grandmothers have known for centuries: Chicken soup is good for colds. Chicken soup contains ingredients that affect the body's immune system, especially due to its anti-inflammatory properties. This might explain why it soothes sore throats and makes you feel better when you have a cold or the flu.

Researchers have found that chicken soup helps stop the movement of neutrophils, white blood cells that eat bacterial and cell debris and that are released in great numbers by viral infections like colds. Neutrophils stimulate the release of mucus, so stopping their movement is a good thing.

In addition to all these amazing things, researchers suggest that the TLC associated with homemade chicken soup can also have a positive effect on the recipient's health—just one more example of how grandma knows best.

fig. A | bring the water and chicken to a boil

fig. B | simmer for 30–40 minutes

fig. C | remove chicken when cooked through

fig. D | add the boned chicken to the veggies and broth, then season

6 **BRING TO JUST UNDER A BOIL, THEN LOWER HEAT.**
Simmer for approximately 10 minutes, or until carrots are tender. A knife should easily pierce the carrots.

7 **WHEN THE CHICKEN IS COOL, REMOVE THE MEAT FROM THE BONES.** Shred it with two forks.

8 **RETURN THE MEAT TO THE SOUP UNTIL IT IS HEATED THROUGH.** Salt and pepper to taste. (Fig. D)

9 **LADLE THE HOT SOUP INTO BOWLS AND SERVE.**
Accompany it with a crusty bread, if you have some.

10 **REFRIGERATE ANY REMAINING SOUP.** If your friend plans on eating the soup within the next week or less, put it in the fridge in a well-sealed container. If he'd rather save it for the next time he's sick, put it in the freezer in a well-sealed container. It'll keep for about a month.

25 SIMPLE WAYS TO DO GOOD WITH FIRST AID

1. Keep a few Band-Aids in your wallet. They'll come in handy.
2. Keep a thermometer, aspirin, and first-aid cream in your desk drawer at work for coworkers who are ill.
3. Offer to pick up prescriptions for someone who can't get out of the house.
4. Be sensitive to those with allergies: Keep your pets in a different room when people with allergies are visiting.
5. Carry sunblock to share with others caught in the sun.
6. Grow an aloe plant and keep it handy in case of accidental burns.
7. Make emergency-contact cards for each member of your family, in case of accident.
8. Learn basic water rescue techniques for times when a lifeguard may not be available.
9. Stow a first-aid kit in your car.
10. Accompany friends on visits to the eye doctor—everyone forgets how difficult it is to function with dilated pupils.
11. Always offer to do a deer-tick check for friends and family after walking in the woods.
12. Carry tissues in your bag—you never know when they'll come in handy.
13. Donate crutches and canes that you no longer need to

hospitals or rehabilitation centers.

14. Post poison hotline numbers at the office and at home.

15. Carry pots of lip balm to share with friends and family whose lips become chapped.

16. Wait hand-on-foot for a sick friend; she'll return the favor when you're sick.

17. Keep ice packs in the freezer just in case.

18. Take a CPR class and keep your certification current.

19. Massage sore muscles or sudden muscle cramps for friends.

20. When camping or attending a theme park, take note of first-aid stations. Point them out to family and friends.

21. Drive elderly friends and neighbors to the doctor, and offer support after the appointment.

22. Become the office fire captain: Ensure that there are extinguishers on every floor, that the fire system is in working order, and that everyone has been educated on evacuation procedures.

23. Remember the power of human touch: give hugs often.

24. Don't hesitate to call the paramedics when a situation is out of control.

25. Remember that humor really is the best medicine: tell jokes!

2

DOING GOOD FOR
FRIENDS & NEIGHBORS

HOW TO GET A CAT OUT OF A TREE

Be aware that sometimes the hero should be a professional arborist, who's comfortable climbing trees. But if none is available, here's how to do it yourself.

1 DON'T PANIC. If the cat was able to climb up the tree, it is likely it will be able to climb down the tree. The cat will not climb down if the commotion to coax it down scares it; often, a cat will descend on its own at night when no one is around.

2 TRY TO ENTICE THE CAT DOWN. Place edible treats in low-hanging branches or at the base of the tree. The cat may climb down willingly for the treats.

3 FIND THE CAT'S OWNER. The presence of the owner and her reassuring voice may help calm the cat. Remind the owner that shouting will not help.

KITTENS

If the cat is only a kitten, it should be rescued immediately. Kittens like to climb to the tops of trees but lack the weight or strength to remain in the tree for long periods of time. A strong breeze may dislodge and injure the kitten. Cats usually land on their feet, but kittens do not.

4 **IF THE CAT STILL REFUSES TO CLIMB DOWN THE TREE, YOU MAY NEED TO CLIMB UP.** Be aware of your own personal safety and health—if you are afraid of heights or have shoulder pain, for example, you may not be the best person to attempt the rescue.

TREE-CLIMBING TIPS

★ *DO NOT CLIMB A DEAD TREE. Dead limbs may break unexpectedly, and they are not safe.*

★ *SURVEY THE TREE AND SURROUNDING AREA FOR HAZARDS. Trees entwined with power lines are hazardous and should not be climbed.*

★ *KEEP AN EYE OUT FOR OTHER ANIMALS IN THE TREE. Although most animals will run when you get close, squirrels protecting their nests and raccoons living in the hollow of a tree may be dangerous.*

★ *IF YOU DO NOT HAVE A LADDER, ALWAYS REACH FOR BRANCHES AT THEIR CROTCH. Maintain a three-point hold (for example, have both feet and one hand stable as you reach for another branch).*

★ *DO NOT LOOK DOWN WHEN YOU BEGIN YOUR DESCENT.*

Fig. A | offer the cat a treat

Fig. B | place the cat in a pillowcase and gently lower it to the ground

5 **BEFORE CLIMBING, GET KITTY TREATS, A PILLOWCASE, AND A ROPE.**

6 **OBTAIN A LADDER.** Place the base of the ladder on level ground and lean it against the trunk of the tree (not a branch). If the ladder is an A-frame, ensure that it is stable.

7 **WHILE CARRYING THE TREAT, PILLOWCASE, AND ROPE, CLIMB THE LADDER.**

8 **WHEN YOU ARE WITHIN REACH OF THE CAT, OFFER IT A TREAT.** Speak gently and reassuringly—you do not want to frighten the cat. Usually, the cat will come to you willingly. (Fig. A)

9 **WHEN THE CAT IS CLOSE TO YOU, SCOOP IT INTO THE PILLOWCASE.** Be gentle, but know that the cat will not like this. Hold the opening closed and tie it with the rope. Slowly lower it to the owner below; instruct her to open the bundle indoors. (Fig. B)

10 **DESCEND THE LADDER.**

OH TANNENBAUM . . .

Cats love to climb Christmas trees, so make sure the tree cannot tip over easily. Either firmly anchor the base of the tree or secure the top of the tree to the ceiling, a piece of furniture, or window treatment with a strong string, wire, or fishing line.

There are also many ways to dissuade the cat from getting near the tree. You could put aluminum foil at the base of the tree, install motion detectors that give off a noise when activated, place mats that give a mild electric shock at the base of the tree, or spray your cat with a water bottle when it gets too close.

HOW TO ARRANGE A BOUQUET OF FLOWERS

Arranging a bouquet is an art form that can take years to learn. If you don't have years to devote to it, here are some simple steps to ensure that your bouquet brings a smile to someone's face.

1 PICK THE MOST CAPTIVATING FLOWER AS THE FOCAL POINT OF THE BOUQUET. Find bright, large flowers that have some "oomph," such as Gerber daisies or lilies. (Fig. A) If the flowers are very large with wide stems, you may not be able to accommodate more than three in the arrangement. Set these flowers aside.

2 CHOOSE A VASE OR OTHER CONTAINER. Ideally, the vase should complement your focal flower. If the flower is tall, pick a tall vase. If the flower is short, a small vase will work well. If possible, choose the color of the vase with the flower's color in mind.

3 PICK SOME SMALL FLOWERS THAT WORK WELL WITH YOUR EYE-GRABBING FLOWER. These flowers' colors should contrast with the main flowers. Choose an odd number of each of these types of flowers to achieve optimal balance.

4 **PICK ENOUGH GREENS TO FILL OUT THE VASE.**
Find greens with an interesting texture. Bushy and leafy is good.

5 **FILL THE VASE TWO-THIRDS OF THE WAY WITH WATER.** Some flowers prefer a specific water temperature—ask a florist about the type of flowers you have chosen. If you have a mixed bouquet or do not know for sure, use lukewarm water. (Fig. B)

6 **ADD FLOWER FOOD TO THE WATER.** This will keep the flowers looking healthy longer. Most flower food is similar in make-up to lemon-lime soda, with an added antibacterial agent to keep the stems open so the flowers receive all the water they need. If you do not have store-bought flower food, substitute a few table-spoons of a lemon-lime soda, a few tablespoons of sugar, a few tablespoons of chlorine bleach—or all three at once. The acidity of the soda lowers the pH so the water is inhospitable to bacteria; the chlorine bleach kills bacteria on the stems; and the sugar provides nourishment. (Fig. C)

Fig. A | pick a captivating flower

Fig. B | fill the vase 2/3 with water

Fig. C | add food to the water

Fig. D | arrange the bouquet

7 **TRIM THE STEMS.** To prolong the life of cut flowers, experts recommend cutting the stems while they are submerged in cold water. This way the cut remains hydrated and the stem is primed to take in water—if you cut the stem out of water, the end dries out, blocking the water. Fill a small bowl with cold water and submerge the stems. Use a sharp knife or pair of scissors to cut the stems at an angle.

TULIP TIPS

Tulips are the only flowers that continue to grow once they are cut. One old wives' tale recommends putting a penny in a vase with tulips, so the copper will keep the stems straight. Experts say this is useful only if you have just cut the flowers from your garden. If you buy the flowers at a retail store, it is too late for the copper to be of use.

8 **BUILD YOUR BOUQUET.** Begin by putting your greens in first. This will give your bouquet structure and keep things in place. Strategically place the smaller "fluff" flowers, one type at a time, evenly throughout the vase. Lastly, find just the right focal point for the big flowers, and place them. For a dramatic look, cluster all the focal flowers together in the center, surrounded by the "fluff" flowers. Or for a more even, balanced arrangement, distribute the bigger flowers throughout, placing them nearest the smaller flowers that contrast the most. (Fig. D)

9 **GIVE AND ENJOY.**

HOW TO SEW ON A BUTTON

A friend approaches you in dismay. The button on her favorite shirt has fallen off. "No problem," you say. "I can help." Knowing how to sew on a button is an infinitely useful skill for helping a friend in need. (Time to brush up on your middle-school home-ec lessons . . .) These directions are for a standard two- or four-hole button.

1 **LOCATE A REPLACEMENT BUTTON.** If you can find the original button, you're all set. If not, you will probably be able to find a replacement. Men's shirts often have extra buttons sewn on at the bottom. Women's shirts often come with extra buttons attached to the price tag in a small envelope. You invariably will have put this button away in case you need it and now can't find it.

2 **IF YOU CANNOT FIND A REPLACEMENT BUTTON, TRY TO IMPROVISE.** Look at the piece of clothing: are there any buttons that aren't really needed, like a shirt button that gets tucked into pants? If not, search your sewing kit (if you have one), pilfer a button from another piece of clothing, or, if you have the time, make the journey to a fabric or sewing store. (Take the

piece of clothing with you to ensure the new button will match.)

3 **FIND THE ORIGINAL LOCATION OF THE MISSING BUTTON.** Look closely at the garment. There should be some torn threads where the button once was or tell-tale holes in the fabric where the threads once were.

ANATOMY OF A SEWING KIT

All adults should have a sewing kit on hand for sewing emergencies. If you want a fancy sewing case, go for it, but a shoe box works just as well. Just make sure you have the following:

* *a couple of needles*

* *a few spools of thread (at least black and white)*

* *a few emergency buttons (include the ones that come with new clothing)*

* *a packet of straight pins*

* *good scissors*

---

4 **CLEAN UP THE SITE.** Get rid of torn threads by cutting them and pulling them out. Take care not to cut the fabric.

5 **THREAD A NEEDLE.** Choose thread that is similar in color to the thread you removed. If you cannot match the color, find a color similar to the garment or button so it will fade into the background. (If the other buttons weren't sewn on with thread of the same color you will be using, sew a bit of the new thread through the other buttons so that they all look the same.) You will need about ten inches of thread for the button. Pull one end of the thread through the eye of the needle until both sides are the same length. Tie both ends into a simple knot at the bottom. (Fig. A)

6 **SECURE THE THREAD TO THE FABRIC.** Start from the back of the fabric (the side you can't see). Take your needle up through the fabric. If the thread pulls right through the fabric, knot and all, make another knot atop the first one and try again.

7 **DETERMINE WHETHER THIS BUTTON IS DECORATIVE OR FUNCTIONAL.** If the button is decorative, it should be sewn tightly against the fabric. If it will be used, create a "shanked" button. A shank is a short stem

that holds a sewn button away from the fabric—
shanks are often made out of thread, though some
special buttons have a shank of plastic or other sturdy
material built-in. The next steps describe how to sew
on a shanked button.

8 **LAY A MATCH ON TOP OF THE BUTTON, BETWEEN THE
HOLES.** Your stitches will pass over the top of the
match before they go back down to form the shank
and ensure that you will have some space for actual
buttoning. You can also use a toothpick or another
needle if those are handy.

9 **BRING THE THREADED NEEDLE UP THROUGH ONE OF
THE HOLES IN THE BUTTON.** (Fig. B)

10 **BRING THE THREAD OVER THE MATCH AND DOWN
THROUGH A SECOND HOLE AND THE FABRIC
BENEATH.** If the button is a four-hole, decide if you
want two parallel lines of thread or an X when choos-
ing which hole to go through. Come back up through
the first hole and repeat three times. (Fig. C) End with
the thread at the back of the fabric. If the button is a
two-hole, move on to step 12. If the button is a four-
hole, go to step 11.

fig. A | thread a needle

fig. B | bring the needle through the fabric and button

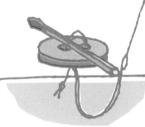

fig. C | repeat the stitch 3 times

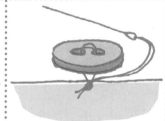

fig. D | bring the thread through the fabric, but not the button

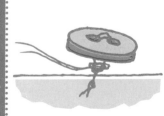

fig. E | wind the thread to make the shank

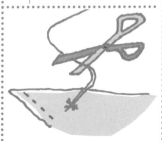

fig. F | trim away excess thread

11 **BRING YOUR NEEDLE AND THREAD UP THROUGH THE THIRD HOLE OF THE BUTTON AND DOWN THROUGH THE FOURTH.** Repeat three times to secure this connection. End with the thread at the back of the fabric.

12 **SLIDE THE SPACE-HOLDING MATCH OUT.**

13 **GENTLY PULL THE BUTTON AWAY FROM THE FABRIC SO THE STITCHES ARE TAUT AND THERE IS A SPACE BETWEEN THE BUTTON AND THE FABRIC.** (FIG. D)

14 **MAKE THE SHANK.** Pull the needle through the fabric, but not through the button. Wind the thread around the threads connecting the button to the fabric four or five times. (Fig. E) Push the needle back through the fabric and tie a knot on the back of the fabric.

15 **TRIM AWAY THE EXCESS THREAD.** (Fig. F) The button is now ready for wear.

HOW TO FIX A ZIPPER

There's nothing worse than arriving at the office and having a zipper break. Repairing a broken zipper takes time, spare parts, and more than a little bit of tailoring skill, but heading off an embarrassing situation can simply be a matter of preparation. If you carry a few safety pins with you at all times, you can save someone's day.

★ **IF THE ZIPPER WON'T CATCH ON BOTH SIDES OR CAN'T BE RAISED AT ALL, USE SAFETY PINS TO CLOSE THE GAP.** Hold the sides of the fabric together as tightly as possible and pin them closed. To keep the repair discreet, it is best to pin from the inside.

★ **IF THE ZIPPER WORKS BUT REPEATEDLY SLIDES OPEN, USE A SAFETY PIN TO ATTACH THE TOP OF THE ZIPPER TO THE FABRIC OF THE PANTS.** There's usually a small hole at the end of the zipper's tab. Catch the safety pin in this hole and then secure it through the fabric near the top of the zipper.

★ **IF NO SUPPLIES ARE AVAILABLE, FASHION A COVER-UP.** A long jacket, a sweater tied around the waist, or an untucked shirt are all possibilities.

HOW TO SOOTHE A FUSSY BABY

Crying, wriggling, and overall unhappiness is a fact of life for most babies. As a friend or family member, you will provide a lifeline if you can soothe and calm the wailing "sweet-pea." Here are some tried-and-true techniques.

★ **DANCE WITH THE BABY.** Any dance steps that are smooth and repetitive are calming. Ideally, your dance steps will include up and down (Fig. A), side to side (Fig. B), and back and forth (Fig. C) motions. Nearly any music will do, but the softer the better.

Fig. A | move up and down

Fig. B | move side to side

Fig. C | move back and forth

* **WEAR THE BABY.** A baby carrier is an extremely useful fuss-prevention tool. Baby slings, or any other carrier in which the baby is physically close to you, will do the trick. Constant touch often miraculously soothes fussy babies, and research shows that babies who are carried more cry less. Some babies may find relaxation with a pacifier while in motion.

* **DRIVE THE BABY.** Put the child in a car seat and hit the road. The monotonous sound of the engine, the vibrations, and the movement will often put a grumpy baby right to sleep.

* **SWING THE BABY.** A gentle, constant swinging motion can sometimes settle an upset baby. Note, though, that mechanical swings are one of the most commonly recalled infant products. Be sure to buy a swing approved by the Juvenile Products Manufacturers Association.

* **TAKE THE BABY ON A WALK.** The movement may calm the baby, and will certainly calm you. Try holding the baby in different positions (over your shoulder or in a cradle position) until you find the perfect spot. Walk around the block, or even stay inside the house.

★ **ROLL THE BABY.** Lay the baby onto his or her belly on a beach ball or exercise ball. While supporting the baby, gently roll the ball from side to side. This rhythmic motion and the new position may distract and calm the baby.

★ **MAKE GENTLE NOISES AT THE BABY.** Soothing, rhythmic sounds with a humming quality work the best. Singing a medley of lullabies, running the vacuum cleaner, or turning on a faucet are all easy options. Be creative, testing out different noises until you find the one that does the trick.

★ **DISTRACT, DISTRACT, DISTRACT.** Try visually stimulating the little one. Make faces. Lay the baby under a moving ceiling fan. Remember that babies love to look at themselves in the mirror.

HOW TO VISIT SOMEONE IN THE HOSPITAL

Hospitals are intimidating places. They bring to mind the frailty of life. When someone you care about is sick and in the hospital, he may feel afraid, lonely, or simply bored. If you follow these basic rules, your visit will go smoothly, and you will truly brighten his day.

★ **FOLLOW ALL HOSPITAL RULES.** Remember that all the rules in a hospital are developed to best serve the patients.

★ **WASH YOUR HANDS.** Before you approach the patient, wash your hands thoroughly. The last thing the patient needs is germs from the outside world.

★ **DON'T VISIT IF YOU ARE SICK OR IF YOU HAVE BEEN EXPOSED TO SOMEONE WHO IS SICK.** Your stuffy nose or hacking cough could jeopardize the patient's health. Also, if you feel fine but your son has the chicken pox, stay away!

★ **DON'T WEAR PERFUME.** Heavy perfume can make even the healthiest people feel sick.

* **CLEAR ALL FOOD YOU WISH TO GIVE THE PATIENT WITH THE PATIENT'S DOCTOR OR THE NURSE ON DUTY.** Even if the patient is having a craving, it may not be good for him to indulge. Don't ever give the patient any medication, alcohol, or other drugs.

* **DON'T STAY TOO LONG.** Decide how long to stay by talking to the patient and his medical providers. Provide support, but don't wear the patient out. If this is a simple well-wishing visit, stay only a few minutes, especially if there are closer friends or family members there.

* **DON'T BRING A WHOLE POSSE.** Too many visitors can be exhausting, and patients are likely to tire easily. A visit from the whole high school football team is only a good idea in the movies.

* **DON'T SIT ON THE BED.** Unless a loved one specific-ally asks you to, don't cramp the patient or invade personal space.

* **TALK CLEARLY.** If the patient is taking medications or is in pain, his mind may be a little foggy. Adjust your volume accordingly.

YOUR FRIENDSHIP IMPROVES HEALTH

In 1988, epidemiologist James House, Ph.D., reviewed studies regarding friendship and health involving more than 22,000 men and women. He found that people with well-established support systems had far longer life spans than those without such support. People with few friends and little support had a death rate two to four times that of people with strong support systems. It's proof that friendship matters. And when your friends are sick, they need you the most.

★ **WHEN YOU GREET THE PATIENT, SOFTLY TAKE HIS HAND.** A soft touch communicates warmth and caring. A strong hug can do real damage to someone who is sick or has recently had surgery. Be gentle.

★ **IF YOU BRING A GIFT WITH YOU, MAKE SURE IT IS RIGHT FOR THE PATIENT.** Don't bring a book for someone who has had eye surgery. Don't give a coloring book to someone who has broken his dominant hand. Find out if the patient is allergic to flowers before bringing them, and if you do bring flowers, bring a vase, too. (Most hospitals don't have enough.) Take the time to arrange the flowers nicely (see "How to Arrange a Bouquet of Flowers," page 42)—chances are that no one else will have the time to do so.

★ **DON'T TRY TO "ONE UP" THE PATIENT.** Be sympathetic, and respect the ills of the person you are there to see. If the patient needs to talk about what he or she is going through, be present and be focused. Validate how hard being sick is.

★ **IF A MEDICAL PROVIDER COMES IN TO CARE FOR THE PATIENT, MAKE A QUICK EXIT.** Give the patient his privacy, unless you are explicitly asked to stay.

hold a hand, give some flowers, sit and talk, or just be there

★ **RESPECT PATIENT CONFIDENTIALITY.** Don't talk about the patient as you ride the elevator in the hospital or as you are waiting in the hall. Everyone deserves privacy.

★ **WASH YOUR HANDS.** Hospitals are full of germs— don't risk getting sick yourself.

★ **TAKE CARE OF YOURSELF.** If being at the hospital upsets you or if seeing this person unwell is hard for you, find someone to talk to when you leave. You need to be well to care for someone who is unwell. Give yourself whatever time you need.

♠ HOW TO HELP A FRIEND QUIT SMOKING

Tobacco use is the leading preventable cause of death in the United States. Each year, more than 400,000 people (one out of every five) die as a result of using tobacco. Smoking kills more people each year than AIDS, alcohol, drug overdoses, car crashes, murders, suicides, and fires combined. That's the bad news. Here's the good news: People who quit smoking immediately reduce their risk of tobacco-related disease, slow down the progression of already established tobacco-related disease, and increase their life expectancy. This is true even when the smoker stops after the age of 65! You can help. Your support can mean the difference between someone simply trying to quit and someone succeeding.

★ **OFFER YOUR FRIEND YOUR UNCONDITIONAL SUPPORT WHILE SHE TRIES TO QUIT.** Your friend does not need hostile confrontation, threats, put-downs, nagging, or preaching. Shaming a smoker is not at all helpful. Build your friend's ego and work to impart the message that she can take control. Remember that smokers must want to quit for themselves, not for anyone else.

★ **GATHER A GROUP OF SUPPORTERS.** If it is okay with

your friend, let her other friends know of her desire to quit smoking. This will ensure that her environment is supportive of this decision as well.

★ **LISTEN TO YOUR FRIEND.** Try to understand what quitting is like for her. Encourage her to determine what kind of help she will need to quit. (Fig A)

★ **HELP YOUR FRIEND FIND HER MOTIVATION.** There are lots of good reasons to stop smoking. Help your friend find the one that is most important to her.

★ **CHEERLEAD.** Offer praise and encouragement every step of the way. Mean it. Send your friend cards with words of encouragement. Call her to tell her that you're proud of her efforts. (Fig B)

★ **LAUGH OFTEN.** Use your sense of humor, and help your friend keep a sense of humor as well.

★ **JOIN IN.** As a show of moral support, agree to give up something that you really love, like chocolate, TV, alcohol, or coffee.

★ **MAKE YOUR FRIEND A SURVIVAL KIT.** You could include carrot sticks, gum, hard candy, toothpicks,

snacks, or games to help her get through each
moment, each day. (Fig C)

★ **IF APPLICABLE, SHARE YOUR EXPERIENCE.** If you
have successfully quit smoking, share your story.
Remember that what worked for you may not work
for your friend.

★ **PROVIDE TANGIBLE INCENTIVES.** Develop short-term
incentives that will work for your friend. For each
milestone (for example, a smoke-free day, a smoke-free
week, etc.), treat your friend to something enjoyable
(good food, good music, good road trip).

★ **CELEBRATE.** Quitting for good is a momentous
achievement. Show your friend that you are proud,
happy, amazed, and in awe of what she has accom-
plished. Throw a big party for her, or make her a
commemorative plaque. Do something to honor the
end of a long, hard process. (Fig. D)

Fig. A | listen to your friend

Fig. B | cheerlead

Fig. C | prepare a kit of snacks

Fig. D | celebrate your friend's success

WHAT WORKS?

Part of supporting a smoker is encouraging the most effective strategies for quitting. Studies have shown that these five steps, if done from start to finish, will help the smoker quit for good. Share them with your friend.

1 GET READY. Plan to quit. Set a date and change the environment (e.g., get rid of ashtrays, discard unused cigarette cartons, etc.).

2 GET SUPPORT AND ENCOURAGEMENT. Tell the important people in your life that you are going to quit and that you want their support. Seek counseling. Connect with a good medical provider.

3 LEARN NEW SKILLS AND BEHAVIORS. Distraction is the best medicine. Change your routine. Do something—anything—other than smoke.

4 GET MEDICATION AND USE IT CORRECTLY. Some medications are proven to help you stop smoking and decrease nicotine cravings. Talk with your medical provider about which one is right for you.

5 BE PREPARED FOR RELAPSE OR DIFFICULT SITUATIONS. Most relapses occur within the first three months of quitting. Don't be discouraged if you start smoking again. Remember, most people try several times before they finally quit.

HOW TO COMFORT A FRIEND

There are times in life when tragedy befalls someone you know. When it does, your friend needs a friend. You may feel awkward in this role, wondering, "What do I say? How do I make the pain go away?" There are no easy answers, but the following simple steps may make all the difference.

★ **SIT WITH YOUR FRIEND.** Sometimes the simple act of sitting in close proximity can be comforting. Your responsibility is to bear witness to your friend's pain, not to offer magic words to take it away. Try not to worry about saying the "wrong thing." If you are nervous, this will only add to your friend's stress. Allow yourself to simply be with your friend.

★ **WALK WITH YOUR FRIEND.** The stress of trauma or grief may physically deplete your friend. Take him or her by the hand and walk, if possible. (Fig. A) Breathe together. The increased blood flow through your friend's body will increase his ability to cope. Again, no words are necessary: Your closeness is a comfort.

★ **GET YOUR FRIEND A GLASS OF WATER.** When a person experiences a loss or great sadness, he is likely to forget to drink. Dehydration can make anyone feel sick, weak, or distraught, and will decrease an individual's ability to cope. Pour a glass of anything without alcohol or caffeine, which will dehydrate! (Fig. B)

★ **MAKE A MEAL.** Along with forgetting to drink, your friend may forget to eat. As blood sugar drops, he will feel woozy and less able to cope. Fix a sandwich, order a pizza, or toss a salad for your friend. (Fig. C)

★ **HELP YOUR FRIEND SLEEP.** The loss of sleep that often accompanies a difficult time will make it even harder for your friend to handle sadness. Fluff a pillow or wash some sheets. (Fig. D) Ask others to keep the noise to a minimum. Sing a lullaby. Hold a hand.

★ **STAY FOR THE LONG HAUL.** Many folks offer help at the time of a crisis. A true friend still comes by one month, six months, or one year later. Be supportive for as long as your friend needs you.

★ **KNOW WHEN TO GET HELP.** If your friend is unable to drink, eat, or sleep, and you are concerned about his health, encourage him to call a doctor. Medical attention may be necessary.

Fig. A | walk with your friend

Fig. B | get your friend a glass of water

Fig. C | make your friend a sandwich

Fig. D | fluff your friend's pillow

25 SIMPLE WAYS TO DO GOOD FOR FRIENDS & NEIGHBORS

1. If a coworker or neighbor is planning a vacation, offer to water plants, house sit, or pet sit.
2. Occasionally bake a friend or coworker's favorite dessert and bring it to him.
3. Send thoughtful cards through the mail—people need to be reminded that they're loved.
4. Offer to walk the dog of an elderly neighbor or friend.
5. Remember the interests of a coworker—even something as simple as clipping an article she may find interesting shows thoughtfulness.
6. Offer to help a coworker with a difficult project.
7. When a friend is in need, do whatever legwork is necessary: Call a lawyer friend for advice, do some research, or even just make time to sit and listen.
8. Surprise a loved one with a gourmet meal—either homemade or a special evening out.
9. Once in a while—not often—unexpectedly drop by a friend's home. Just chat a while. A short face-to-face visit can brighten someone's day.
10. If a neighbor is out of town and a heat wave comes on, water his lawn.
11. Check in on elderly neighbors regularly.

12. Organize a carpool for bringing your kids and their friends to school.
13. Send friends little gifts for minor holidays: first day of spring, Labor Day, and especially Valentine's Day.
14. Make or buy cookies for the office.
15. Don't overstay a welcome.
16. Offer to go grocery shopping if a neighbor is unable to do so herself.
17. After trash pickup, carry your neighbor's empty cans up to his house for him.
18. Call an old friend out of the blue.
19. Offer to take a friend's children out for an afternoon or evening so that he or she can have some time alone.
20. Offer to help friends move.
21. Deliver a casserole or dessert and lists of local restaurants, grocery stores, hardware stores, and other points of interest when a new person moves into the neighborhood.
22. Introduce yourself to all of your neighbors—it's always good to be friendly.
23. E-mail virtual greeting cards to people "just because."
24. When you see a moving truck on your block, volunteer to help carry boxes. You may befriend a new neighbor or get to say one last farewell to an old one.
25. Remember your friends' birthdays, and send a card or make a call to wish them well.

3

DOING GOOD FOR
STRANGERS

HOW TO JUMP-START A CAR

If you have ever been stranded in a car with a dead battery, you know the power of a jump-start. When some kind soul drives up with jumper cables, it's like seeing a person in a red cape and tights. You can achieve instant superhero status by keeping jumper cables on hand and following these simple steps.

1 PUT ON A PAIR OF GLOVES. There is acid in batteries, and it's best to be safe by keeping your skin protected.

2 MAKE SURE THE CAR NEEDS A JUMP-START. Check that the car's battery cables are tight and that the battery posts are clean. If they aren't, clean and tighten the dirty and loose cables. (Sometimes that's all that is wrong.) Next, look at the battery. If the battery is cracked or broken, the car needs a new battery; if it has been extremely cold, the battery might be frozen. Don't jump a cracked or frozen battery—it might explode. Call a mechanic instead.

3 CONSULT THE OWNER'S MANUAL. The manual should have all the details for jump-starting that particular car. It is always best to read the car manufacturer's directions first. The directions that follow, however, are general enough that they can apply to any car.

4 **POSITION YOUR CAR SO THAT IT IS FACING THE BROKEN-DOWN CAR, HOOD TO HOOD.** The distance between vehicles must be short enough that the jumper cables can reach each car's battery, with enough space for you to maneuver. Make sure that the cars aren't touching each other.

align the cars near each other, hood to hood

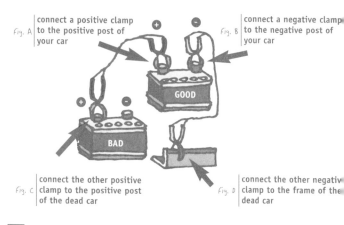

Fig. A connect a positive clamp to the positive post of your car

Fig. B connect a negative clamp to the negative post of your car

Fig. C connect the other positive clamp to the positive post of the dead car

Fig. D connect the other negative clamp to the frame of the dead car

5 **TURN OFF BOTH CARS' ENGINES.** Turn off all lights and unplug radar detectors and cell phones. Make sure that both cars are in park.

6 **CONNECT THE POSITIVE (USUALLY RED-HANDLED) CLAMP TO THE POSITIVE BATTERY POST ON YOUR CAR.** This post will have a (+) marking on it or next to it, as will the clamp. The positive terminal on a battery is always larger than the negative terminal. (Fig. A)

7 **CONNECT THE NEGATIVE (USUALLY BLACK-HANDLED) CLAMP TO THE NEGATIVE BATTERY POST ON YOUR CAR.** This post will have a (-) marking on it or next to it. (Fig. B)

8 CONNECT THE REMAINING POSITIVE CLAMP TO THE POSITIVE BATTERY POST ON THE CAR WITH THE DEAD BATTERY. (Fig. C)

9 CONNECT THE REMAINING NEGATIVE CLAMP TO THE ENGINE OR FRAME OF THE CAR WITH THE DEAD BATTERY. (Fig. D) Don't connect the clamp directly to the battery. When you make the last connection, it could cause a spark, and the battery might explode. Look for an unpainted area some distance away from the battery. Try a bracket or bolt. Make sure the clamp is secure.

SAFETY TIP: Batteries release explosive gases and can be very dangerous. Never smoke while charging a battery!

10 RESTART YOUR CAR.

11 START THE CAR WITH THE DEAD BATTERY. If the car doesn't start ("turn over"), check the cable clamps to make sure you have a good connection. (If the broken-down car still won't start, you may need to consult a mechanic.)

12 REMOVE THE JUMPER CABLE CLAMPS IN THE REVERSE ORDER THAT YOU ATTACHED THEM.

13 LEAVE THE ENGINE OF THE FORMERLY DEAD CAR RUNNING FOR AT LEAST HALF AN HOUR TO CHARGE THE BATTERY.

YOUR BEST BET

Even though jump-starting someone else's car with your own is a very simple and common task, it is not without risk. If done incorrectly, you could damage your car or the other person's. You may want to purchase a "jumper box" (also called a "booster box"). This box can jump-start a car without using a live battery—just charge it up at home, and you can stow it in the trunk for as long as one year without recharging. When you find a vehicle in need, simply connect the cables that come with the box, turn it on, and the broken-down car will have enough battery power to get to the nearest auto repair station. Jumper boxes are inexpensive and available at most autoparts stores.

HOW TO CHANGE A FLAT TIRE

There's nothing worse than hearing the pop and hiss of a tire gone flat. If you come across an unfortunate soul who has had a blow-out, follow these steps to help him on his way.

1 MOVE THE CAR TO A SAFE POSITION. Safety is of utmost importance. If the car is not in a good spot, ask the driver to move it. Find a place close by where you are as visible as possible, especially if it is dark. Stay as far away from traffic as possible while still being on a level surface. Driving on a flat tire increases the risk of damaging it even further, so settle on the first good spot available.

2 TURN ON THE EMERGENCY OR "HAZARD" LIGHTS.

3 SET THE EMERGENCY OR PARKING BRAKE. Cars with automatic transmissions should be in park. Cars with manual transmissions should be in first gear or reverse. Find two large rocks and put them in front of and behind the tire opposite the flat. (For example, if the driver's side front tire is flat, place the rocks around the passenger's side front tire.) This will decrease the chance of the car rolling and potentially injuring you.

4 **PROTECT YOUR HANDS.** If you have gloves with you, put them on.

5 **FIND THE SPARE TIRE AND JACK.** Get out the owner's manual for a diagram of the car. (Fig. A) You will usually be able to remove the spare by unscrewing whatever bolts hold it in place in the trunk or, in a truck, under the bed.

AN OUNCE OF PREVENTION . . .

Take a moment right now to think about a flat tire—now, not when you are stuck on an interstate. Being familiar with your car and equipment will help you fix not only your own car but others as well.

★ *FIND YOUR SPARE TIRE. It is usually on the floor of your trunk. Make sure it is properly inflated and easily accessible.*

★ *FIND YOUR CAR'S JACK. The jack is most likely made of metal and is triangular.*

★ *FIND YOUR LUG NUT REMOVER. The lug nut remover (also called a lug nut wrench or tire iron) that came with your car is probably pretty useless. Buy one that is shaped like a cross, with three different-sized sockets and a pry end. Make sure that one of the sockets fits your car's lug nuts securely.*

---

6 **USE A LUG NUT REMOVER TO LOOSEN THE LUG NUTS AROUND THE FLAT TIRE.** Do this before you jack up the car—it's easier. There are usually four or five lug nuts near the center of the wheel. They may be hidden underneath a hubcap or some sort of plate that you will need to pry off. Turn the lug nuts counterclockwise to loosen them, but don't remove them just yet.

7 **JACK UP THE CAR.** Place the jack six to twelve inches behind a front flat tire or six to twelve inches in front of a rear flat tire. (Fig. B) Raise the jack until it just touches the car, then position the jack exactly where you need it. Each car manufacturer has a special place for the jack to contact the car, so check the owner's manual. Ensure that the jack is flat against the ground. Once the jack is securely in place, crank it until the car rises about six inches off the ground.

8 **REMOVE THE OLD TIRE.** Remove the previously loosened lug nuts. You should be able to do this by hand. Put them in a spot where you won't lose them. Grab the tire with two hands and pull it straight off. (Fig. C) Keep your legs apart and stabilized as you crouch down so that you don't fall over.

9 **PUT ON THE SPARE TIRE.** It may take a little bit of shimmying to get the spare lined up correctly. Align the holes in the center of the spare with the threaded shafts they fit over. Push the spare in as far as it can go.

10 **REPLACE THE LUG NUTS.** It is important that you do this correctly: Take the lug nuts and screw them on the shafts with your hands. Use your lug nut remover to get them flush to the tire, but don't tighten them yet.

11 **GENTLY LOWER THE JACK UNTIL THE TIRE IS JUST TOUCHING THE GROUND.**

12 **FINISH TIGHTENING THE LUG NUTS.** Tighten one of the lug nuts with just one turn of the wrench. Then do the same to the lug nut opposite that one. Now do the rest the same way. Repeat, jumping from lug nut to opposite lug nut until each one is tight. This ensures that they are tightened evenly. (Fig. D)

13 **LOWER THE CAR THE REST OF THE WAY.** When there is no longer weight on it, the jack will fall over. If you removed a hub cap or plate, put it back by holding one edge in place and banging on the opposite edge with the lug nut remover.

Fig. A | gather together the supplies

Fig. B | place the jack near the flat

Fig. C | remove the flat tire

Fig. D | finish tightening the lug nuts

HERE I COME TO SAVE THE DAY

*If you have just come upon someone who needs help chang-
ing a tire, feel free to puff out your chest, put your hands on
your hips, and say in a confident voice, "Don't worry, I'm
here to help."*

*Do whatever you can to let the person with the flat know
that you are not a predator, but ascertain that the person
with a flat is not a predator either. There is no simple formu-
la for doing this. You will need to rely on your gut instinct.
Taking stock of your surroundings will help: Is the area well-
traveled? Are you in a safe, visible spot? Are you near a
town?*

*If you want to help but are a little wary, your best bet is to
call the state police/highway patrol. (Nothing wrong with
getting a little back-up.) You can let the stranded motorist
know that you have already called the police for help but
that you will help change the tire. This will assuage your
fears and, perhaps, his.*

14 **PUT AWAY THE JACK AND THE FLAT TIRE.** Put the jack
back where you found it. Put the flat tire where the
spare once was.

15 **IT IS NOW SAFE FOR THE OWNER TO DRIVE THE CAR.**
There is a limit to how long it is safe to drive on a
spare. Riding on a spare tire for an extended period

could damage the car. Encourage the driver to get a new tire as soon as possible. Service stations should be able to help.

16 **TAKE A MOMENT TO FEEL GOOD.** You did it! Bask in the glow of your accomplishment.

HOW TO HELP A PERSON CROSS THE STREET

When helping others, be sensitive to and respectful of the other person's feelings. If you were in need of assistance, you'd want others to remember that you're still a competent person—you just need a helping hand. Remember this the next time you see someone who looks like she might need help crossing the street, whether she's elderly, blind, or disabled. Ask yourself: Does this person need my help? Does this person want my help? Try following these simple steps for guidance.

1 **STAND A FEW FEET AWAY FROM THE PERSON YOU THINK NEEDS HELP.** Everyone wants her personal space to be respected. Even if she can't see you, she can smell you, hear you, or sense that you are there.

If the person is blind and using a guide dog, be sure not to pet the dog. You may be aching to nuzzle its neck, but this dog is working and should not be distracted.

IT'S THE LAW

Only individuals who are blind may carry white canes; in all 50 states the law requires drivers to yield the right of way when they see a blind person's extended white cane.

2 OFFER YOUR ASSISTANCE.
Be straightforward. Say,
"Would you like some
help crossing the
street?" If she says
no, that is her prerog-
ative. Be polite.

**3 IF THE PERSON WOULD
LIKE HELP, ASK HER HOW
YOU CAN BEST ASSIST.** Don't make
any assumptions about what would be useful. Never
grab the person's arm. She may just want you to walk
beside her or carry her bag.

**4 WHEN YOU ARE SAFELY TO THE OTHER SIDE OF THE
STREET, ASK IF SHE NEEDS ANY FURTHER ASSIS-
TANCE.** You may ask, "Are you all set?" The person
may appreciate assistance carrying heavy bags to her
home. If the person is blind, she may want you to
describe any potential hazards in the vicinity or provide additional support.

HOW TO GIVE GOOD DIRECTIONS

Being able to give clear, concise directions is an invaluable skill. Sure, the Internet can give you quick and easy access to destination-specific maps, but it is of no use when you are traveling down unfamiliar roads in an unfamiliar area, yearning for a friendly face willing to give good directions. You can be that friendly face. Just follow these simple rules the next time someone asks you for directions.

★ **BE HONEST.** If you don't know how to get to a destination, don't venture a guess. Direct the driver to a nearby gas station, if possible.

★ **BE SPECIFIC.** Use clear words to state exactly what you mean. For example, don't say, "You'll pass through a couple of lights" when you mean the driver will pass through two lights.

★ **TRY TO NOTE THE MILEAGE BETWEEN POINTS IF YOU KNOW IT OR CAN MAKE A REASONABLE GUESS.** It is helpful to know that you will be on a road for one mile, five miles, or 15 miles before you embark on your journey so you know when you may have gone astray.

★ **INCLUDE AS MANY LANDMARKS AS POSSIBLE, BUT DO NOT CLOUD THE PICTURE WITH LANDMARKS.**
Landmarks let people know they are on the right track. You can say, "Take a right after the synagogue. You'll pass the park on your left. Turn right at the high school. The library will be on your left." But don't list every shop, tall tree, and street sign along the way. Just a few that can be easily remembered will do.

★ **OFFER A MAP IF YOU'VE GOT ONE.** You can highlight the route on the map with a pen or pencil.

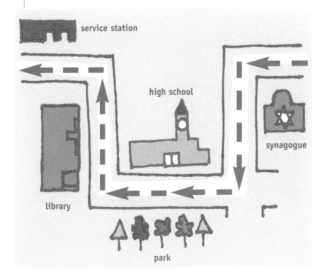

* **MENTION LANDMARKS THEY WILL PASS IF THEY MISS THEIR MARK.** For example, "If you pass the service station, you've gone too far."

* **HAVE COMPASSION.** Be kind. You never know when the roles will be reversed and it will be you seeking a kind soul to guide you to your destination.

HOW TO TAKE A PHOTO FOR STRANGERS

Tourists visiting new places will inevitably want a photograph to commemorate their visit. Often, they'll ask a stranger standing nearby to take a picture of their group—and in doing so, they entrust that stranger to take a decent picture. Prove your mettle by following these steps to give a visitor happy memories.

1 **FAMILIARIZE YOURSELF WITH THE CAMERA.** Ask the owner to show you how to focus (if necessary), click the shutter, and zoom.

2 **MAKE SURE THE SETTINGS ARE CORRECT.** If the light is dim, find out if the flash will go off automatically. Ask the owner to set the camera up exactly as he'd like it. If the camera is not automatic, make sure the film has been advanced.

3 **ASK THE OWNER WHAT ORIENTATION TO USE— LANDSCAPE OR PORTRAIT.** Hold the camera at the outer edges to ensure your fingers don't cover up the lens. Remember that on most automatic cameras the viewfinder does not look directly through the lens, so even if you do not see your finger when looking through the camera, this doesn't mean you aren't inadvertently covering the lens. Keep the camera horizontal if they'd like a landscape shot; turn it vertically to take a portrait shot.

4 **ASK THE OWNER WHAT ELEMENTS HE WANTS IN THE PICTURE.** If there is a landmark in the background, find out if he wants the entire object or just a particular element. Ask if he'd like his group pictured from the waist up or from head to toe, and if he would like the group off to one side or centered in the frame.

5 **COUNT TO THREE, TAKING THE PICTURE AS YOU SAY "THREE!"** Even if the tourists are foreign, they will understand these three numbers and will be ready for the picture at "three." Don't take too long to count—approximately one second between each number suffices.

6 **HOLDING YOUR HAND STEADY, PRESS FIRMLY ON THE BUTTON AND LISTEN CAREFULLY.** If the camera is automatic, you should hear the film advance. If the camera is not automatic, you should hear the click of the shutter. If you have reason to doubt the picture's quality, offer to take another.

7 **RETURN THE CAMERA TO ITS OWNER.**

PHOTOGRAPHY 101

★ **THE SUN CAN CAST UNFLATTERING SHADOWS BETWEEN 10 A.M. AND 3 P.M.** *Use the flash to tone down these shadows, or angle your subjects so the shadows don't interfere with the image.*

★ **AVOID PLACING YOUR SUBJECTS DEAD CENTER IN THE FRAME.** *Placing your subjects slightly off to one side creates a more dynamic photo.*

★ **TAKE A MOMENT TO THINK ABOUT THE BACKGROUND OF THE PHOTO.** *Avoid positioning your subject directly in front of a pole or another distracting object; compose the shot to eliminate as much background clutter as possible.*

★ **PEOPLE PHOTOGRAPH BEST WHEN THEY ARE RELAXED AND COMFORTABLE.** *Chances are if you appear relaxed and friendly, your subjects will be more likely to relax for the camera.*

HOW TO FIND A MISSING CONTACT LENS

Contact lenses have an unpredictable habit of leaping out of a person's eye. When the contact gets too dry, an errant blink can knock it out—certainly meriting an emergency response.

1 **CHECK THE WEARER'S EYE TO ENSURE THAT THE LENS HAS REALLY FALLEN OUT.** A contact lens can become "lost" within the wearer's eye by sliding under an eyelid or becoming otherwise displaced. Reassure the wearer that it's physically impossible for the lens to get lost behind his eye. To find the errant lens in the eye, ask the wearer to slowly move his eyes right, left, up, and down. The lens might come back to the correct position on its own. Alternatively, he could close his eye and gently rub the lid in a circle. Before he touches his eye to find the missing contact, suggest that he wash his hands to avoid infection.

2 **IF THE LENS CAN'T BE FOUND IN HIS EYE, CHECK HIS CLOTHING.** Contacts are likely to get stuck on clothing. They can also become entangled in long hair. Carefully scan these areas. Most likely, the contact lens hasn't dried out completely, and the moisture should reflect the light, making it shine a bit.

4 **CHECK THE SOLES OF NEARBY PEOPLE'S FEET.** A lens will stick to the sole of a shoe if stepped on. Ask people around to lift their feet and show their soles to you, so you can determine if the lens is stuck in a tread.

5 **CAREFULLY SURVEY THE AREA.** Some contact lenses have a blue tint and are easy to identify from afar. Carefully scan all furniture and objects near the wearer, and look closely at the floor. If you have a flashlight and are in a room that can be darkened, turn off the lights and survey the area with the flashlight beam. The lens will reflect the light better under darkened conditions.

ALL DRIED UP

When a soft contact lens is exposed to air, it rapidly dries out and will shrink to about one-third its normal size. After about 20 minutes, it becomes brittle—it will feel like a small potato chip—and is easily broken. Be very careful picking up a dry lens. If it is stuck to something, soak it with saline solution before dislodging it.

6 **IF YOUR EYES HAVEN'T SPOTTED THE LENS, TRY USING YOUR SENSE OF TOUCH.** Take off your shoes and socks and slowly walk around the room, using your feet to feel the floor for the lens. The soles of your feet are more sensitive than you think they are. If you're uncomfortable doing this, get down on your hands and knees and use your hands to feel for the lens.

7 **IF THE LENS STILL HASN'T TURNED UP, USE A VACUUM CLEANER WITH A HOSE ATTACHMENT.** Cover the end of the hose with a nylon stocking and secure it with a rubber band. Holding the nozzle one inch above the surface, sweep the vacuum hose over everything: the vacuum will catch the lens and hold it against the nylon.

8 **WHEN YOU FIND THE LENS, TREAT IT GENTLY.** Place the lens in saline solution for at least 30 minutes to rehydrate. Then the wearer can begin his normal process of sterilizing the lens. If saline is not available, use water. If there is no water or saline, saliva will do, but only as a last resort. If the lens looks like it might be damaged, the wearer should take it to a contact lens specialist.

HOW TO HELP SOMEONE OVERCOME A FEAR OF FLYING

Flying is a fast, easy way to travel—you can span great distances in very little time. But flying can be a stressful, difficult proposition for people who have fears of flight. If you are seated on a plane next to someone who is panic-stricken about flying, helping her get through the flight will be the greatest act of kindness she could hope for. And with any luck, she'll be better prepared for dealing with her next flight without you.

1 FIND THE FEARFUL. It is often easy to recognize a fellow passenger who is afraid to fly. More often than not, she will be up-front about her fear, telling you about it from the outset. She may also be giving physical cues, such as gripping the arm rests, breathing quickly, or tightly shutting her eyes on takeoff, landing, or during turbulence.

2 DRAW HER OUT. Before takeoff, strike up a conversation with the seatmate you suspect is afraid to fly. Ask her if she travels often. Usually, a fearful person will open up immediately upon being asked.

SAFETY IN STORMY WEATHER

Being in a plane during a thunderstorm can be unnerving for anyone. Here are some facts to alleviate your seatmate's anxieties (as well as your own).

★ *AIRCRAFT RADAR CAN EASILY DETERMINE THE SIZE AND INTENSITY OF STORMS SO THAT THE CREW CAN PLAN ACCORDINGLY.* Storms won't come as a surprise to the crew.

★ *PILOTS GENERALLY AVOID THUNDERSTORMS, BUT FLYING THROUGH A STORM ISN'T DANGEROUS.* The plane is a completely bonded metallic conductor. This means that a lightning strike would not go through the plane. Being in a plane during thunder and lightning is safe, both in the air and on the ground.

3 LISTEN. It's never a good idea to dismiss someone's anxieties with glib reassurances. Give her a chance to express how she feels—what she is afraid of, what she thinks may help. Listen attentively without interrupting. Often, just expressing her fears can provide a release to the passenger. Acknowledge how hard this experience is for her and tell her that you applaud her courage. Tell her that she is not alone—you are by her side.

4 **HELP THE PASSENGER TRUST THE PILOT, THE FLIGHT CREW, AND THE PLANE ITSELF.** Make sure the flight attendant and the passenger meet. Educate the fearful passenger on the nature of turbulence, or ask a flight attendant to do so. Liken turbulence to a bumpy road—neither will hurt the vehicle.

5 **REMIND THE PASSENGER TO BREATHE.** She may involuntarily hold her breath from anxiety. Suggest she take deep breaths, breathing in through her nose and out through her mouth, which will aid in relaxation and reduce her anxiety. Lead by example. Take deep breaths so that her breathing synchs with your rhythm.

6 **DISTRACT.** Talk about everyday things. Get her focused on something she loves—her family, her job, her hobbies. Ask a constant stream of questions. Bring out a deck of cards, offer the use of your CD player, or share your laptop and play a game. Taking her mind off her fear can go a long way to erasing it.

You look out your window and all you see is snow. Glorious? Yes. Daunting? Sometimes. If someone is house-bound, infirm, or physically unable to shovel snow, a big winter storm can be terrifying. It can be soothing to know that someone cares enough to clear a path to the front door. If you've got a shovel and a little time, why not lend a hand?

1 **DETERMINE IF YOU ARE NEEDED.** If you think a neighbor may need your help and snow is coming, knock on his door or give him a call. Stress the fact that there is no charge. If the snow has already fallen and your neighbor's home is surrounded, call to make sure he'd appreciate your help.

2 **WARM UP YOUR MUSCLES.** Prepare yourself by warming up a bit. Run up and down the stairs a few times. (Fig. A) Stretch your back and legs by touching your toes and twisting from side to side.

3 **DRESS APPROPRIATELY.** Dress in layers to maximize warmth but allow for easy removal if you get hot. Wear a hat, scarf, and gloves. If the sun is out, wear sunglasses. (Fig. B)

4 **STEP OUTSIDE AND PLAN YOUR SHOVELING APPROACH.** First clear a path from the door to the street to provide access to and from the road. If there is a driveway, do that second.

5 **IF THE SNOW IS DEEP, SHOVEL IT IN TWO STAGES.** First shovel the top layer. Set your feet hip-width apart and bend your knees slightly. Face the snow you intend to clear away. Holding the shovel near your body, bend from the knees (not your back) and scoop a layer of snow onto the shovel. (Fig. C) Toss the snow forward onto the ground, away from the path. Don't throw the snow over your back, and don't twist to the side.

> ### WHAT A WORKOUT!
>
> *Shoveling is great exercise— 15 minutes of shoveling snow counts as moderate physical activity, according to the 1996 Surgeon General's Report on Physical Activity and Health. Shoveling is an excellent way to burn calories and get a cardiovascular workout.*

6 **SHOVEL THE LOWER LAYER OF SNOW.** Drop the edge of the shovel down until it hits the cement and scrape the shovel under the snow. Always toss the snow forward. Note: If the snow was not very deep to begin with, you do not need to shovel in two layers.

Fig. A | warm up before shoveling

Fig. B | dress in warm layers

Fig. C | scoop the top layer first

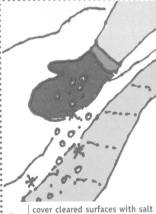
Fig. D | cover cleared surfaces with salt or sand

7 **TAKE FREQUENT BREAKS.** Go inside for a drink of water.

8 **WHEN ALL THE SURFACES ARE CLEAR, COVER THEM WITH SALT OR SAND.** Both will provide traction; the salt will also lower the freezing temperature of the water and keep new ice from forming. (Fig. D)

9 **REWARD YOURSELF WITH A HOT DRINK.**

I'LL MAKE THE HOT COCOA INSTEAD

You are at the greatest risk of having a heart attack while shoveling if you:

★ *have already had a heart attack*

★ *have a history of heart disease*

★ *have high blood pressure or high cholesterol*

★ *smoke*

★ *lead a sedentary lifestyle*

If you meet any of these conditions, it's not recommended that you attempt to shovel. Sit back and make some hot chocolate for the kind soul who clears your walk for you.

---

25 SIMPLE WAYS TO DO GOOD FOR STRANGERS

1. Offer directions or help to strangers who look lost. Often they're too embarrassed or scared to ask.

2. Every once in a while, pay the toll for the people in the car behind you. Chances are, they'll be so surprised and excited, they'll pay for someone else down the road. The good feelings will spread.

3. Offer to carry groceries to the car of an elderly or disabled person while at the grocery store.

4. Leave generous tips for good service. People in service jobs have tough work and get paid very little.

5. When a child drops a toy or bottle, save the parent— whose arms are most likely full—the trouble of getting it by picking it up yourself. Hand the item to the parent, not the child, though, in case the object is dirty.

6. If a child near you on a bus, train, or airplane is being fussy, talk to him. Children will often settle down in a conversation with a stranger. The child's parent and all the other passengers will be grateful.

7. Volunteer at a homeless shelter.

8. Feed a parking meter about to expire.

9. Say "bless you" or "geseundheit" when strangers sneeze. They're always pleasantly surprised.

10. Hold the door open for the person behind you.

11. If you're tall, offer to retrieve things off high store shelves for short people.
12. Give up your seat on a bus, subway, or train to a family with young children, the elderly, or the handicapped.
13. Be patient. This is useful whether you're in line at the Motor Vehicle Administration or at a bus stop.
14. Smile often. People will respond in kind.
15. Volunteer to read to kids at your local library.
16. Thank people often.
17. In a Laundromat or dormitory, occasionally fold the laundry from the dryer instead of piling it atop the dryer.
18. Compliment a stranger: on his tie, on her hair, on his hat.
19. Be a courteous driver, allowing others to merge in front of you or for pedestrians to cross the street before you proceed through an intersection.
20. Offer to share your umbrella with someone in the rain.
21. Clear your table of trash in fast-food restaurants and coffee shops where there is no waitstaff.
22. Allow someone with only a few items to go before you in line at the grocery store, especially if your cart is full.
23. Offer to share your cab with a stranger headed in the same direction.
24. If someone's bag is open and his or her wallet is visible, let him or her know to foil potential pickpockets.
25. Make an effort to return any lost (or stolen) items you may find (e.g., earring or wallet).

4

DOING GOOD FOR YOUR COMMUNITY

HOW TO START A NEIGHBORHOOD WATCH

Neighborhood Watch (NHW) does not require a great deal of time, commitment, or even structure. NHW is simply a group of neighbors willing to watch out for each other and agreeing to call each other and the police if they see unusual activity in the area. It's been said that it takes a village to raise a child—it also takes a village to promote safety and security.

NHW is not a vigilante organization. It promotes awareness techniques and crime reporting rather than physical confrontation of criminals. By deciding to be part of a Neighborhood Watch, you are agreeing to communicate openly with your neighbors and to be aware of what is going on around you. Here's how to start an NHW in your community.

1 **DISCUSS THE NEED FOR AN NHW WITH YOUR NEIGHBORS.** Talk to your neighbors to see if they share your concern.

2 **DECIDE, WITH YOUR NEIGHBORS, WHAT THE BOUNDARIES OF YOUR NHW WILL BE.** What do you consider your neighborhood? Is it just your block or does it encompass a larger area?

3 **CONTACT YOUR LOCAL POLICE DEPARTMENT TO SET UP AN INITIAL MEETING.** Speak with someone who oversees the NHW programs. He or she will help you plan a first meeting. Arrange for a suitable place to hold your first meeting; local churches and schools are usually very cooperative.

4 **ADVERTISE THE MEETING TO YOUR NHW AREA.** Be creative with fliers, go door-to-door within the area, or call the neighbors you know. Let everyone know when and where the meeting will be held. If you don't have access to a computer or copier to make the fliers,  ask your police contact for help. Your police contact will also help you get permanent NHW signs for your neighborhood if you want them.

5 **HOLD YOUR FIRST MEETING.** The first meeting is basically a social event and information-sharing time. The police officer will let your group know how NHW works and how it can help your community.

6 **DURING THE MEETING, SELECT THE NEIGHBORHOOD WATCH DIRECTOR(S).** Ask if there are any volunteers or nominations, then hold a vote. Either a single individual or a small team can fill the NHW director's position. The director has three main responsibilities:

* Acting as the primary contact for the police
* Organizing NHW meetings and information-sharing meetings with the block captains
* Reviewing tips and information on suspected criminal activities in the NHW area and looking for crime patterns or potential suspects

7 **DURING THE MEETING, SELECT THE BLOCK CAPTAIN(S).** You will need one block captain for every ten homes. The block captains have a wide range of simple responsibilities, including:

* Meeting each resident in her assigned area and offering to enroll neighbors in the NHW
* Maintaining an emergency phone list of all her assigned residents
* Being available to pass on information about criminal activities in her area
* Forwarding information to the NHW director and activating the phone tree if she receives information on a suspect in the area.

HOW TO MAKE A PHONE TREE

A phone tree is a list of neighbors with their addresses and phone numbers organized as a flow chart. For an NHW, the director's information would be at the top of the tree, with branches to the block captains. Each block captain would have connections to the ten houses that he or she is responsible for calling.

If something needs to be communicated, the director will activate the phone tree by contacting each of the block captains. In turn, the block captains will call all the people on their branches.

In addition to being a fast and effective way to spread information to many neighbors, the phone tree allows NHW members to contact just one neighbor if necessary.

8 IN THE FOLLOWING WEEKS, THE DIRECTOR AND BLOCK CAPTAINS SHOULD MEET. During their meetings, they can organize the structure of the NHW. They will decide whether the whole neighborhood will meet regularly or not. They can establish rules and guidance for electing NHW directors and block captains and decide how to disseminate information to the neighborhood. They should draft a flier for all members of the neighborhood that describes how to be a member of the NHW.

9 ONCE THE NHW HAS BEEN ORGANIZED, THE DIRECTORS SHOULD HOST A KICK-OFF EVENT FOR THE WHOLE NEIGHBORHOOD. They should pick a location where they can have a small reception with food and drink. The group should invite the area councilperson, the mayor's office, and the police officers who patrol the neighborhood. Information pertaining to the NHW can be distributed, including a short description of the NHW, the phone tree, and other necessary numbers or procedures.

10 WORK WITH THE POLICE TO KEEP YOUR NEIGHBORHOOD SAFE. Communicate with your neighbors. Be aware of your surroundings. Make your NWH work.

HOW TO CONFRONT PREJUDICE

Sadly, racism, sexism, and homophobia pervade our world. This sort of discrimination hurts the victim and demeans those doing the victimizing. Perhaps you've felt helpless when faced with a racist slur, sexist joke, or homophobic comment. Know this: You can make a difference by making sure that you are part of the solution, not part of the problem.

1 DON'T IGNORE IT. Don't let an incident pass without a remark. When you let offensive statements pass you send the message that you are in agreement with such behavior or attitudes.

2 CHOOSE THE TIME AND PLACE TO RESPOND. Your best bet is to follow-up in private. If the comment was made in public, wait for a moment when you're alone with the individual to bring up your concern, maybe while in the car driving home, or suggest that you take a moment away from the group.

> *Always evaluate the security of the situation when confronting prejudice. Ask yourself whether you need back-up to keep you safe or if there is someone better equipped to respond to the situation (e.g., the police). You won't do anyone any good if you get yourself hurt.*

3 **DON'T SHY AWAY FROM TENSION OR CONFLICT.** In
fact, expect it. Remember that tension and conflict
can sometimes produce positive change.

4 **THINK ABOUT WHAT YOU WANT TO GET OUT OF
THE "INTERVENTION."** If a comment or action hurts,
the tendency is to strike back. But tit-for-tat is not
productive. If your goal is to challenge someone's
behavior, be sure not to escalate matters into confrontation or negate his right to speak his beliefs.

5 **PROJECT A FEELING OF UNDERSTANDING, LOVE,
AND SUPPORT.** Without preaching, state how you feel
and firmly address the hurtful behavior and attitude
while supporting the dignity of the person making the
prejudiced remark. Try to assume good will.

6 **USE "I" STATEMENTS, NOT "YOU" STATEMENTS, TO
EXPLAIN HOW WHAT WAS SAID MADE YOU FEEL.** Use
humor when appropriate. Ask questions to help you
figure out the real concern underlying the comment.
Listen closely. Consider that there might be some hurt
motivating the bigoted comment, and respond to it.

7 **BE NONJUDGMENTAL BUT KNOW THE BOTTOM LINE.**
Don't act superior—a patronizing attitude is not

productive. Simply make it clear that issues of human dignity, justice, and safety are nonnegotiable.

PREPARE YOURSELF FOR A LIFE OF STAMPING OUT PREJUDICE

★ **BE AWARE OF YOUR OWN ATTITUDES AND STEREO-TYPES.** *Everyone has biases. Make sure you've examined yours.*

★ **GATHER ACCURATE INFORMATION TO CHALLENGE STEREOTYPES AND BIASES.** *Take responsibility for educating yourself about your own and others' cultures. As the saying goes, knowledge is power.*

★ **DISTINGUISH BETWEEN CATEGORICAL THINKING AND STEREOTYPING.** *Categories help us sort out information and make sense of the world. Acknowledging obvious differences is not a problem, but placing negative values on those differences is—it's called stereotyping.*

★ **BE A ROLE MODEL.** *Reflect and practice nondiscriminatory values in all aspects of your behavior, both personally and professionally.*

★ **TEACH OTHERS THROUGH POSITIVE EXAMPLES.** *Provide examples of individuals whose lives challenge stereotypes.*

♣ HOW TO BE A GOOD WITNESS

It is a colossally bad idea to attempt to arrest someone on your own. Restraining someone physically can result in great harm to you. Furthermore, you may be held criminally or civilly liable for any damage you cause to the suspect. The most powerful thing that you can do to bring a criminal to justice is to work with the law enforcement system by serving as a confident and accurate witness.

1 **NOTIFY POLICE UPON OBSERVING A CRIME.** Contact the nearest law enforcement officials. They are well trained and will know the most effective way to proceed.

2 **PROVIDE POLICE WITH INFORMATION TO ASSIST IN IDENTIFYING THE VIOLATOR.** Note any characteristics of the perpetrator, the time of day, the location of the crime, and any other information that may be relevant. (See "How to Be a Good Observer," p. 118.)

3 **SIGN A COMPLAINT FORM AT THE LOCAL POLICE STATION.** The complaint form, depending on jurisdiction and level of offense, may be a written statement, a taped statement, or an appearance before a judge or magistrate. It will identify you as a witness and will contain your description of the crime and the suspect. The procedure is relatively simple and may take only a few minutes.

4 **COOPERATE COMPLETELY WITH THE POLICE DEPARTMENT AND OTHER LEGAL PERSONNEL.** You may be asked to identify a suspect in a lineup, or be asked to meet with the district attorney's office to testify in the case. You may be required to meet with the defense attorney for a deposition. It's at this point that some people may prefer not to be involved any further, but our legal system won't work without the assistance of ordinary citizens willing to invest their time and energy.

If you come upon someone who is in danger and you need to act quickly to save someone's life (before the police get there), you must decide in a split second if this situation is worth risking your own safety and if you think that you can help. If you can, do it. Scream! Throw things! Honk your horn. Yell "Fire" so that others will come running. Yell, "I've already called the police," even if you haven't. Rally others to intervene with you—most times four people can stop the misdeeds of one. Take action, and don't be a bystander—it's your duty as a good citizen and as a human being.

HOW TO BE A GOOD OBSERVER

★ **STAY CALM.** *Fear and adrenaline often change one's perception of facts and circumstances. This can result in "tunnel vision"—that is, you may be unable to make note of important things happening in your peripheral vision.*

★ **FOCUS ON THE SUSPECT.** *Remind yourself that you will have to identify this person at a later date. Try to lock the suspect's physical appearance in your memory. (Fig. A)*

★ **FOCUS ON THE INDIVIDUAL FROM HIS OR HER HEAD DOWN.** *Pretend you are going to draw this person later. Notice how big each feature is in relation to the others. Notice any characteristics that stand out (e.g., scars, tattoos, etc.). (Fig. B)*

★ **NOTICE THE SUSPECT'S MODE OF ESCAPE AND DIRECTION OF TRAVEL.** *If it is in a car, memorize the license plate number. Even one or two letters or numbers and their placement are helpful. Remember the make and model of the car, as well as the color and any identifying marks (e.g., dents) that would help officers searching for it. If the suspect is running, note whether he or she is limping (a limp will greatly affect how quickly the suspect can travel on foot). (Figs. C, D)*

★ **WRITE DOWN A DESCRIPTION IMMEDIATELY.** *As your emotional state changes and your body's adrenaline depletes, your visual memory may change.*

By being a good witness and observer, you're playing an important part in holding the community together and keeping it secure.

fig.A | lock the suspect's physical appearance in your memory

fig.B | notice any characteristics that stand out

fig.C | notice the suspect's direction of travel

fig.D | notice the suspect's mode of escape

♣ HOW TO BECOME AN ORGAN DONOR

Saving someone's life sounds like a job for a superhero. In fact, it's fairly easy. Each day, approximately 63 people receive an organ transplant, but another 16 people die because not enough organs are available. Individuals waiting for transplants are matched to organs by blood and tissue typing, medical urgency, time spent on a waiting list, and geographical location. You could be the right match!

1 DETERMINE IF YOU CAN BE AN ORGAN AND TISSUE DONOR. Talk to your doctor to find out if it would be safe for you to donate an organ. Some people can give up one kidney without any adverse effects, but for others, it's not a good idea. If you wish your organs to be donated after your death, it's likely that there won't be a problem. Some religions do not condone organ donation, however, so speak with your clergy before signing a donor card or pursuing the donation.

2 TALK WITH YOUR FAMILY MEMBERS AND LOVED ONES ABOUT YOUR DECISION. Take the time to talk to the important people in your life about your wish to be an organ donor. It is important that your family knows how you feel about this issue. Make sure they know that it will not cost them anything. All hospital and medical costs associated with the donation are paid for by the organ or tissue recipient, usually through insurance. If the donation will happen after your death, they may be comforted to know that the donation will not interfere with the kind of funeral or memorial they would want to have for you.

> **SHOW ME THE MONEY?**
>
> *No way. The National Organ Transplant Act makes it illegal to sell human organs and tissues.*

3 **IF YOU KNOW THE PERSON YOU WISH TO DONATE TO, FIND OUT IF YOU ARE A MATCH.** Your doctor can perform the necessary tests to determine if you can donate to this person. Talk with your doctor about any potential risks. Find out if the donation will require major life changes on your part.

4 **IF YOU ARE CLEARED TO DONATE TO A SPECIFIC PERSON, BE PREPARED FOR THE SURGERY AND ANY OTHER PROCEDURES.** Make sure you understand what will happen and what you will need in order to recuperate. You're giving the best gift of all, but not without some work on your part. You deserve some special treatment as well.

5 **IF YOU WISH TO ALLOW YOUR ORGANS AND TISSUE TO BE DONATED AFTER YOUR DEATH, INDICATE IT IN WRITING.** You will be given this option when you renew your driver's license. In addition, you can call your local Organ Procurement Organization to get a copy of an organ donor card or whatever form your state uses.

6 **CARRY YOUR ORGAN DONOR CARD (OR ITS EQUIVA-LENT) WITH YOUR DRIVER'S LICENSE.** Your intent to be a donor will be noted on your driver's license. Keep your signed commitment (if applicable) with your license at all times.

WHAT'S RACE GOT TO DO WITH IT?

In organ and tissue donation, race and ethnicity matters. Some diseases of the kidney, heart, lung, pancreas, and liver are found more often in racial and ethnic minority populations than in the general population. For example, African Americans, Asian and Pacific Islanders, and Hispanics are three times more likely to suffer from end-stage renal disease than Caucasians. Native Americans are four times more likely than Caucasians to suffer from diabetes. As a rule, a patient's body is less likely to reject donated organs if they are from an individual who is genetically similar. Thus it is vital that individuals of all races contribute to the pool of donor organs.

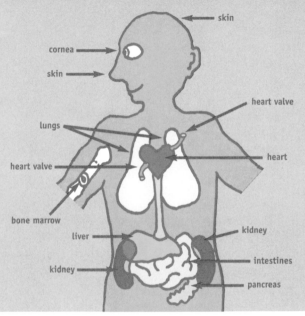

There are so many organs and tissues needed by so many people. There is a good chance that you have an organ that someone out there can use. Organs that can be donated include the heart, kidneys, pancreas, lungs, liver, and intestines. Donatable tissues include the cornea, skin, heart valves, and connective tissue. You can also donate your bone marrow, a kidney, or a segment of your liver or lung while you are living. If you are willing to donate only some things and not others, you can indicate this on your donor card.

♣ HOW TO DONATE BLOOD

Seven percent of the human body is made up of blood. It is our life force, moving nutrients, oxygen, and vitality. Donating blood is one of the simplest ways to do good for friends and strangers alike. Each donation can save as many as three lives.

1 **DETERMINE IF YOU CAN GIVE BLOOD.** Most people can. You must be at least 17 years old, but there is no upper age limit. You must be healthy, so if you are battling an illness yourself, it is not a good time to give blood. You must weigh at least 110 pounds, and you must not be pregnant. If you donated blood within the last 56 days or donated double red cells in the last 112 days, you'll have to wait a little longer before you can donate again. If the American Red Cross or any other blood collection organization tells you not to give blood, determine another way to help out. (For more specifics, see "Who Should Not Give Blood," p. 128.)

2 **DECIDE WHERE YOU WANT TO GIVE BLOOD.** Join a local blood drive; locations and times are often listed in your local newspaper. You can also call the American Red Cross (1-800-GIVE-LIFE) or go to their Web site (www.redcross.org) to find your local chapter, which will know the location of the donation center nearest you. If you prefer, call your local hospital, which will most likely welcome you with open arms.

PLATELET APHERESIS

Most patients undergoing a bone marrow transplant, surgery, chemotherapy, radiation treatment, or organ transplant at some point need platelets in order to survive. Platelets have only a five day storage life, so they are used almost immediately after donation. Until recently, the only way to get enough platelets for a transfusion was to pool blood donations from five to ten donors, separate the platelets from the other blood cells, and then combine the platelets. Now, new technology—blood cell separators—can collect enough platelets from one donor using a technique called apheresis.

Blood is drawn from a donor, the blood goes through a blood cell separator, platelets are removed, and the rest of the blood is returned to the donor into the same vein or into a vein in the other arm. This process is simple and safe, though it requires more time than whole blood donation (about two hours). Within 48 hours, your body will replenish the platelets (which means you can donate again every 48 hours but no more than 24 times a year).

3 DO IT. Donating blood is a four-step process that usually takes a little more than an hour.

* **REGISTRATION.** A reception desk attendant will help you fill out necessary forms and get you on the list for the phlebotomists (the people who draw the blood) to call.

* **INTERVIEW.** You'll be asked some very personal questions. This information is private and confidential. Depending on your answers, you may be asked not to donate, either temporarily or permanently (see "Who Should Not Give Blood," p. 128). You will also receive a mini-physical exam that includes a check of your temperature and blood pressure. You should tell your interviewer if you aren't feeling well or if you have a fever.

* **DONATION.** All of the supplies in this process, including the needles, are used only on you, and only one time. The phlebotomist will clean off an area of your arm to get it ready. Then you'll feel the sting of the needle—it only lasts a couple of seconds. Collecting your blood only takes about eight to ten minutes.

  First the phlebotomist will seat you in a reclined chair. After swabbing the inside of your elbow with a sterile disinfectant, the phlebotomist will tie a rubber tourniquet around your upper arm and may ask you to squeeze your hand into a fist. The tourniquet and squeezing action will pump blood to your arm and increase the size and visibility of the veins.

The needle the phlebotomist will insert is already attached to the tubing and collection bag—it's a completely closed system. You may be asked to continue squeezing until the bag is full. You can relax when the phlebotomist indicates that you've donated enough. After the tourniquet is released, the needle will be removed and direct pressure will be applied to the donation site with sterile gauze. To prevent bruising, you will be asked to sit with your arm elevated.

You are losing only a pint of blood, and your body will replace the plasma (the liquid part) in just a few hours and the cells in a few weeks. If you feel faint, tell the phlebotomist immediately.

★ **RECOVERY.** Relax. Lie down or just sit still, whatever feels best. Enjoy a little bit of free orange juice and cookies and feel good about what you did. Most people feel fine after donating blood, but some may experience an upset stomach, a black and blue mark at the injection site, or dizziness. If you experience these symptoms, let the folks around you know and take it easy for a while. You will leave the donation

WHO SHOULD NOT GIVE BLOOD

Note: This list does not cover every possible cause for deferral, and criteria can change. Check the Red Cross Web site or contact your local blood bank.

You should not give blood if you have:

* *gotten a tattoo within the last 12 months*

* *ever had or are at risk for Creuzfeldt-Jakob Disease, or if any blood relative has had it*

* *ever received a dura mater (or brain covering) transplant during head or brain surgery*

* *received an injection of bovine (beef) insulin made from cattle in the United Kingdom since 1980*

* *had hepatitis on or after the age of 11*

* *had malaria in the past three years*

* *lived in the United Kingdom for a total of three months or in Europe for a total of six months since 1980*

* *been held in a correctional facility for more than 72 straight hours in the last 12 months*

* *been to Cancun or Cozumel in Mexico or taken a Caribbean cruise in the past 12 months.*

* *had or been treated for syphilis or gonorrhea, or tested positive for syphilis in the last 12 months*

* *been raped in the last 12 months*

* *inhaled cocaine or another street drug in the last 12 months*

* *contracted AIDS or one of its symptoms*

* *done something that puts you at risk for becoming infected with HIV, the virus that causes AIDS.*

site with additional information on caring for yourself as well as a number to call in case you realize
after you leave that your blood may not be safe.

4 **AFTER YOU DONATE, YOUR BLOOD WILL BE TESTED
EXTENSIVELY BEFORE IT IS GIVEN TO ANOTHER PER-
SON.** The site where you donated blood will notify you
if tests show you may be unhealthy.

5 **TELL A FRIEND.** This is a case where peer pressure is a
good thing. Tell all your friends about how easy it is
to donate your blood. Spread the word!

HOW TO PLANT A TREE

Trees clean the air, shelter birds, provide shade, and make the planet a green, lush place. Humans simply can't live without them, so plant one and make the world a better place!

1 DECIDE WHERE YOU WANT TO PLANT THE TREE. This will help you figure out what kind of tree you want to plant. Think about sun and shade—big shady trees go well on the south side of the house; in the summer their leaves cast shade, but in the winter they allow strong sunlight in. If you have an empty space on your property, you may want to fill it with a tree.

2 FIND OUT IF THE AREA YOU CHOSE IS SUITABLE FOR A TREE. Look to see if there are any utilities in the area. Most cities will send someone out to locate underground utilities for you at no cost. Next, figure out what the area is like for the roots. Check the drainage.

3 DETERMINE HOW TALL YOU WOULD LIKE THE TREE TO GROW. If you want shade on a second-story window, you will need a larger tree. You'll also need to ensure that there is enough space for a large trunk.

Remember that trees will get larger as they grow older, so determine if the tree will eventually encroach on the house, the sidewalk, your driveway, or any other important feature of your home.

4 **GET PERMISSION FROM THE POWERS THAT BE.** If you are planting on public land, you may need to get permission from whomever manages public space in your area. If you are planting on your own land, then the "powers that be" may just be Mother Nature.

5 **BUY THE TREE.** You may be able to get a tree donated for your project if it is being planted on public land. Ask your state or community forest representative to see if

> *Look for the following to find a strong, healthy tree:*
> * *A good, strong trunk with no cuts or scrapes*
> * *A decent size "root ball" (a.k.a. ball of roots), with no kinked roots*

there are any programs that sponsor tree giveaways. If you're selecting a tree at a nursery, tell a salesperson about the conditions at your proposed planting site and why you want the tree in order to pick just the right kind.

6 **TRANSPORT THE TREE TO THE SITE.** Handling a tree and moving it around will cause the tree some stress, so be gentle. If it is just a sprouted seed, you will not have to do much to protect it in transit, but if it is a young tree, ensure that the root ball is wrapped in clean burlap or otherwise protected. Secure it on your vehicle so that it will not move during the journey.

7 **USE A SHOVEL TO DIG A HOLE.** Make the hole slightly deeper than your root ball and about three times as wide. If the hole is too deep, the roots won't have access to enough oxygen. If the hole is too narrow, the roots won't be able to expand to get enough nourishment or provide a strong base for the tree. Don't pat down the soil inside the hole. If the interior of the hole is too smooth (called "glazing"), water won't be able to reach the tree.

8 **REMOVE ANY CONTAINER OR BURLAP COVERING THE ROOT BALL AND LOOSEN THE SOIL AROUND THE ROOTS.** Think of the roots as the tree's blood vessels. They work best when they are not twisted or knotted. Set them free, using a knife or pruner. If the root ball was in burlap and you can't get it all off, don't worry about it. (It will turn into organic matter over time.) Always be careful not to damage the root ball, and don't leave your root ball lying around where it can dry

out or be damaged—
plant it in the ground
as soon as possible.

9 **PLACE THE TREE IN
THE HOLE.** You don't
want to plant too
deep—this can kill the
tree over time. The
majority of the roots on
the newly planted tree
will develop in the top
12 inches of soil. It's better
to plant the tree slightly high (one to two inches
above the base of the trunk flare) than to plant it
at or below the original growing level.

AND THE SEASONS, THEY THEY GO ROUND AND ROUND

When is the best time to plant a tree? New trees do best in mellower weather with moderate temperature. They need time to get their bearings before the heat of summer or the cold of winter comes along. For most of us, that means spring or early fall are the best planting times.

10 **FILL IN THE HOLE.** Have another person hold the tree
straight. Pack the soil carefully so that there are no
air pockets. To do this, add the soil a few inches at a
time and settle each layer with water before adding
more soil.

11 **WATER THE TREE.** Give it a good soak the first time
around. After that, your tree will need about two to
three gallons of water each week for the first year.

(Hopefully, Mother Nature will take care of most of the watering for you.)

12 **MAKE YOUR TREE A BLANKET OF MULCH.** Create a two- to four-inch covering of rotten leaves, wood chips, pine straw, or shredded bark. Cover the entire area you dug up, starting a few inches out from the base of the tree. This will insulate the ground, keep moisture at the roots, provide your tree with needed nutrients, and keep weeds to a minimum.

13 **TAKE A MOMENT TO SAVOR YOUR HANDIWORK.** Maybe a picnic? A smooch? A photo? You have done something worthwhile on behalf of Mother Nature and all who inhabit the planet, so take a moment to revel in it.

fill in the hole while a friend holds the tree straight

25 SIMPLE WAYS TO DO GOOD FOR YOUR COMMUNITY

1. Organize a community garden if there is no other place for people to grow flowers or plant vegetables.
2. Write to your elected officials to voice your concerns; begin a letter-writing campaign for pressing issues.
3. Vote. At every election.
4. Volunteer at a local elementary school—the teachers always need helpful hands.
5. Organize a carpool to work—you not only reduce air pollution, but you take the driving stress off others on a regular basis.
6. Volunteer to coach a sport, either at the junior, middle, or high school level.
7. Plan a block party so neighbors have time to meet one another.
8. Donate food to shelters on a regular basis—not just around the holidays.
9. Clear your closet of good-quality clothing you no longer wear and donate it to a shelter.
10. Give money to local charities. Even $10 goes a long way.
11. Learn to knit hats for your hospital's preemie ward; one hat doesn't take long to make, and it'll keep a newborn warm and cozy in an otherwise uninviting environment.

THE GOOD DEED GUIDE

12. Organize a neighborhood street cleaning.
13. Don't stand by idly while someone litters—confront the person and remind him that we all share these spaces, so keep them clean.
14. Learn about recycling opportunities in your community and make sure they are being correctly utilized.
15. Save energy by turning off lights when you leave a room and running air conditioners infrequently.
16. If you have a friendly pet, see if the local hospital uses animal therapy—find out if your pet can pass the test to comfort sick patients.
17. Clean up after your dog. Leaving a mess is illegal and disgusting.
18. Report downed trees and potholes so they can be repaired.
19. Get involved in local politics.
20. Support school fundraisers—even if you don't buy something, donate a few dollars to the cause.
21. Walk or bicycle to work.
22. Support community activities by attending events in parks or fundraisers held by community organizations.
23. Become a mentor to a younger child.
24. Sponsor a house party or concert with benefits going to charity.
25. If you see suspicious behavior, immediately call 911.

EXPERTS

DOING GOOD WITH FIRST AID

How to Help an Injured Bird
Holly Seitz, public relations and marketing coordinator, The Tracey Aviary, Salt Lake City, Utah.

How to Treat a Child's Skinned Knee
Anthony Compagnone, M.D., fellow of the American Academy of Pediatrics, Hyde Park Pediatrics, Boston, Massachusetts.

How to Remove a Splinter
Anthony Compagnone.

How to Cure Hiccups
Matthew Danigelis, M.D., Department of Emergency Medicine, Hennepin County Medical Center, Minneapolis, Minnesota.

How to Save Someone Who Is Choking
Matthew Danigelis.

How to Make Chicken Soup for a Sick Friend
Bob Shuman, owner, Zaftigs Delicatessen, Brookline, Massachusetts.

DOING GOOD FOR FRIENDS AND NEIGHBORS

How to Get a Cat out of a Tree
Robin Massanti, animal control officer, South Windsor Police Services, South Windsor, Connecticut. Michael Martinez, expert tree climber, Specialized Rigging and Tree Care, Inc., West

Roxbury, Massachusetts.

How to Arrange a Bouquet of Flowers
Catherine "Cat" Thompson, owner, Petal and Leaf Florist, Jamaica Plain, Massachusetts.

How to Sew on a Button
Janet Grace, retired home economics teacher, South Windsor, Connecticut.

How to Fix a Zipper
Janet Grace.

How to Soothe a Fussy Baby
Anthony Compagnone.

How to Visit Someone in the Hospital
Allan Goldblatt, M.D., executive director, Patient Care Assessment Committee, Massachusetts General Hospital, Boston, Massachusetts.

How to Help a Friend Quit Smoking
Michael Solomon, M.D., second-year fellow in Pulmonary Critical Care, Georgetown University Medical Center, Washington, D.C.

How to Comfort a Friend
Steven Gross, M.S.W., program director, The Trauma Center Community Services Program, Boston, Massachusetts.

DOING GOOD FOR STRANGERS

How to Jump-Start a Car
Rob and Fred Morrison, Morrison's Autorite, Jamaica Plain, Massachusetts.

How to Change a Flat Tire
Rob and Fred Morrison.

How to Help a Person Cross the Street
Patricia Maurer, director of Community Relations, National Federation for the Blind, Baltimore, Maryland.

How to Give Good Directions
Dennis Callahan, owner, City Cab Company of Waltham, Massachusetts.

How to Take a Photo for Strangers
Andrea Stephany, photographer, Philadelphia, Pennsylvania.

How to Find a Missing Contact Lens
Joanna Giddon Mandell, contact lens wearer for 20 years. N. F. Burnett Hodd, an ophthalmology practice in London.

How to Help Someone Overcome a Fear of Flying
Jeanne McElhatton (founder) and Captain Mark Connell, board members, Fear of Flying Clinic. Capt. Connell is also a United Airlines pilot.

How to Shovel Snow
Melissa Mangham, www.applesforhealth.com; Donna B. Yeaw, www.donnabyeaw.com, freelance writer.

DOING GOOD FOR YOUR COMMUNITY

How to Start a Neighborhood Watch
Sergeant Matthew Reed, manager of Crime Prevention Services, South Windsor Police Department, South Windsor, Connecticut.

How to Confront Prejudice
Lindsay Friedman, director, A World of Difference Institute,

How to Be a Good Witness
Sergeant James Goldblatt, Naples Police Department, Naples, Florida.

How to Become an Organ Donor
Mary L. Ganikos, Ph.D., chief, Education Branch, Division of Transplantation, Office of Special Programs, Health Resources & Service Administration, Rockville, Maryland.

How to Donate Blood
Rita A. Reik, M.D., F.C.A.P., senior medical officer, American Red Cross National Headquarters, Washington, D.C.

How to Plant a Tree
Cindy M. Stachowski, International Society of Arboriculture certified arborist, chief operating officer, National Tree Trust, Washington, D.C.

VOLUNTEER RESOURCES

ACTION WITHOUT BORDERS
www.idealist.org

Action Without Borders is a global network of individuals and organizations working to build a world where all people can live free and dignified lives. The Web site is the richest community of nonprofit and volunteering resources on the Web, with information provided by over 29,000 organizations in 153 countries, and thousands of users every day.

CARE 2 MAKE A DIFFERENCE
www.care2.com

This online organization has partnered with The Nature Conservancy and The Wildlife Conservation Society to benefit environmental causes.

THE CHRONICLE OF PHILANTHROPY
www.philanthropy.com

An online newspaper for the non-profit world, containing articles on various volunteering opportunities.

CITYCARES
http://cares.org/national

This is the Web site for the parent group of local organizations providing volunteer recruitment in 24 cities.

INDEPENDENT SECTOR
www.indepsec.org

A Web site for a national nonprofit organization that supports philanthropy and volunteerism.

MAKE A WISH FOUNDATION
www.wish.org

The Web site for a foundation that focuses on making wishes come true for children coping with life-threatening illnesses.

NATIONAL SERVICE-LEARNING CLEARINGHOUSE
www.servicelearning.org

A source of information about and resources for service-learning programs, which combine service to the community with student learning.

PEACE CORPS
www.peacecorps.org

The Web site for the Peace Corps, an organization that is committed to serving people around the world.

POINTS OF LIGHT FOUNDATION
www.pointsoflight.org

The Web site of the organization that engages people in volunteer community service to help solve serious social problems.

THE RED CROSS
www.redcross.org/volunteer

The Web site for the Red Cross, the country's leading resource for medical aid worldwide.

VOLUNTEER MATCH
www.volunteermatch.org

An online service devoted to helping interested volunteers become involved with their communities by matching location and interests with volunteering opportunities.

ABOUT THE AUTHORS

James Grace is a legal services attorney who is currently the Executive Director of Volunteer Lawyers for the Arts of Massachusetts, Inc. He is the co-author of *The Worst-Case Scenario Handbook: Golf* and *The Art of Spooning* (with his wife, Lisa).

Lisa Goldblatt Grace is an independent consultant providing technical assistance and training to programs serving teen parents throughout the United States. She holds masters degrees in social work and public health. Her past work experiences include directing a shelter for homeless teen moms and serving as co-director of a diversion program for youth offenders.

James and Lisa are raising their daughter, Avery, and their son, Cooper, in Jamaica Plain, Massachusetts, a land of many good deeds.

ACKNOWLEDGMENTS

We'd like to thank all the experts who did a good deed by donating their time and resources to this project. We also wish to thank our editor, Erin Slonaker, and David Borgenicht for making this book happen. We are enormously thankful to our family and friends, who embody goodness and caring. Finally, we thank the woman who jump-started our car on a hot day in Wellfleet, the mom who made macaroni and cheese for our kids when we were camping and ran out of food, and the countless other strangers who have done good deeds for us.

6/6/03